As We
Grow Old

As We Grow Old

How Adult Children and Their Parents Can Face Aging with Candor and Grace

RUTH FOWLER

Judson Press ® Valley Forge

As We Grow Old: How Adult Children and Their Parents Can Face Aging with Candor and Grace
© 1998 by Judson Press, Valley Forge, PA 19482-0851

Bible quotations in this volume are from the New Revised Standard Version of the Bible, copyright 1989 by the Division of Christian Education of the National Council of the Churches of Christ in the U.S.A. Used by permission. All rights reserved.

Library of Congress Cataloging-in-Publication Data
Fowler, Ruth.
    As we grow old : how adult children and their parents can face aging with candor and grace / Ruth Fowler.
        p. cm.
Includes bibliographical references.
ISBN 0-8170-1276-1 (pbk. : alk. paper)
1. Aging parents—Psychology. 2. Adult children—Family relationships. 3. Parent and adult child. 4. Retirement—Psychological aspects. 5. Aging—Religious aspects—Christianity.
I. Title.
HQ1063.6.F68 1998
362.6—dc21   97-52170

Printed in the U.S.A.
06 05 04 03 02
10 9 8 7 6 5 4 3

To my loving,
beautiful, warmhearted mother,
who has taught me great
lessons of grace and faith,
and
to my courageous,
intelligent, hardworking father,
whose death could not erase the
power and dignity of his life

CONTENTS

ACKNOWLEDGMENTS

This book is dependent upon dozens of older parents and their children who talked freely with the author about their feelings. Without them none of the rest of the work would have been authentic. Their identities have been disguised by using false names. In addition, several professional counseling and medical sources were consulted and are credited in the references.

Thank you to Dr. Herbert Savel, a physician who has cared for the needs of older adults for many years, and Emilia Taylor, an attorney specializing in trusts and estates, who were helpful in reading portions of the book. A special word of appreciation goes to the parishioners of Westport Federated Church, Westport, New York, where the author served as pastor during her writing of this book, and of Community Baptist Church in Port Dickinson, New York, where she is now pastor, for their support and encouragement.

I used to be a big, strong man. I carried my daughters on my shoulders through the snow and protected them from noises in the night. . . . Now I am old and they don't know what to do with me. They talk in whispers about me and glance at me to see if I'm listening to them. It's as if I were an infestation of unwanted insects. . . . I wish they still thought I hung the moon. It's a lot more fun to be a hero than a burden.

— John, 76, retired school bus driver

I can't get my daughter to understand that I don't want her to take care of me. I know I have limited money. If anyone understands how limited my money is, it's me. But I would rather pay someone to help me afterward [speaking of anticipated knee surgery] than have her helping me to the bathroom and such. You see, I've always taken care of her, and it breaks my heart that she doesn't need me anymore, let alone my feeling like I need her. I need that little bit of dignity; I am still the mother.

— Rebecca, 78, retired farmer

INTRODUCTION

Most of the first lessons adult children learn about growing old come from their parents. Sons and daughters grieve the loss of the vitality, energy, and health of their parents and at the same time gain understanding about the aging process by seeing their parents age. In later years parents continue to teach their children, as these younger adults watch how their older parents cope with their changing physical and mental status.

Often adult children see in their parents one possible vision of their own future, and this can be both a frightening experience and an educational one. Parents who maintain an active relationship with God and continue to have faith in the grace of Christ in the face of troubling changes are able to give every generation in their family lessons in faith and grace in the face of difficulty. As they enter their middle years, sons and daughters look at postretirement parents. In this culture the burden of care seems to shift from parents caring for children to children caring for parents. This book focuses on what the aging process means for both generations.

The postretirement age group popularly called "older adults" now spans thirty years. The changes faced during that time are often frustrating and can become uncontrollable and dehumanizing. Older parents and their adult children, some in this postretirement group themselves, face adjustments in relationships and care arrangements, which can be challenging, uncomfortable, and sometimes heartbreaking.

Communications between these two generations often become strained with misunderstanding. Adult children are not always able to hear and understand the needs and concerns of their older parents. Likewise, older parents can misunderstand their children's desires and goals. Often the two generations clearly understand each other but have opposing goals and ideals. Communication is hampered not only by the emotional charge of the parent-child relationships but also by the stereotypes and wrong perceptions some of the culture holds about growing old and older persons.

Not all older parents are alike. Most older adults maintain a high level of independence and health until the time of their death. They may never need the responsibility of their care to rest anywhere but with themselves. Adult children can face a delicate decision about when and if to intervene in their parents' care. Many children ask themselves again and again over the years, "How much care does my mother (or father) need?"

Older parents may resist adapting to changing circumstances, especially those that involve increased dependence on children or increased loss of privacy and dignity. Their resistance is often aimed at their children in what feels to the children like personal hostility. It is more likely that these older parents are simply trying to continue to control their lives as best they can. In the most severe instances the problem of elder abuse and neglect arises. Physical abuse and neglect may be present, but financial abuse and psychological abuse through the violation of basic rights are more likely. Financial abuse includes the taking of property and possessions without permission or necessary legal authorization and misusing property. Some adult children assume that their parents' property belongs to them. Psychological abuse of elders includes threats to abandon them or to place them in a nursing care facility.

Older parents are sometimes self-abusive, primarily refusing food or medical care. In such cases the children may feel unable to help them.

Better understanding between the generations might help prevent some of the problems. The voices and experiences of other older parents, persons who do not share the emotional history of the adult children, are sometimes easier to understand. This book seeks to give older parents a voice by combining interviews, information, and advice to help their adult children better understand their parents and older parents better understand themselves.

Communication and understanding are not only for the well-being of family relationships but they are critical to the well-being of the older parent. Most of the systems that respond to the needs of older parents look to their adult children for guidance and direction when it is felt that older parents can no longer make their own decisions. Medical, financial, and governmental institutions expect parents to become dependent, in varying degrees, upon their children. For older parents to receive the attention and care needed, their adult children must understand their care issues from the older parents' perspective.

It is critical for the well-being of this society that more people listen to older adults and understand their needs and conflicts. This population subgroup is getting larger and larger. The 1990 census statistics indicate that the number of older Americans increased by 5.7 million, or 22 percent, since 1980, compared to an increase of 8 percent for the under sixty-five population. The elderly represented 12.6 percent of this country's population, about one in every eight Americans. Projections are that by the year 2030, there will be sixty-six million older persons, two-and-a-half times the number in 1980 (American Association of Retired Persons [AARP] 1991).

Many of this group are women, who face the multiple jeopardy for discrimination because of age, sex, class, and physical infirmity. Women are poorer throughout their lives, earning less money of their own, and thus are poorer during retirement. Many women currently in the postretirement group have been in dependent relationships for much of their lives and, as they are less able to care for themselves, may become increasingly dependent on their children.

The Select Committee on Aging, U.S. House of Representatives, in *Exploding the Myth: Caregiving in America*, January 1987, reports that the caregiver population, both primary and secondary, is mostly women (Brody and Semel 1993, 40). Seventy-two percent of the caregivers in the country are women; the remaining 28 percent are men. Because women also live the longest, the persons most elderly and in need of care are women. This means that 70 percent of nursing home residents are women; 80 percent of those over seventy-five years of age are women (Grambs 1989, 86).

Older parents discussed in this book range in capabilities from newly retired persons of relative good health and mental capacity to the very elderly who have no ability to care for themselves and have diminished mental capacity. However, all older parents have some factors in common (adapted from Muslin 1992, 2-3):

1. As a group, they are going through physiological and metabolic changes associated with aging that have already or will eventually alter their ability to function. All persons are involved in an aging process, with normal developments for each age group. In older adults the normal developments will include slowing down of body functions, loss of energy, and varying degrees of impairment of vision and hearing. They often find more time for meditation and prayer but are less able to do the activities of church and worship.

2. As a group, older parents have been designated by their cultures as unable to continue as participants in their professions or occupations. This definition ordinarily includes an arbitrary age, such as sixty-five or seventy, which may or may

not reflect the actual abilities of an individual to participate in the workplace. In spiritual life this age group has experienced more, had more tests of faith, and received more blessings than younger generations in their family. Their change of working status can at times be balanced by a new place or role as spiritual mentor.

3. As a group, older parents are experiencing diminished mental capacities as a result of the physiological and metabolic aging processes. Individuals may be experiencing mental disorders in varying degrees associated with adjustments required by aging. In all arenas of older parents' lives, persons need to be able to respond with understanding to the various capacities presented. Some parents have lost short-term memory but can carry the stories of past generations to current children and grandchildren.

As individuals, older parents bring a variety of personal experiences, gifts, abilities, and needs to the wider community. The most common problem faced by older adults is the desire of their broader community to lump them together and assume that they are all alike.

This book strives not only to show the common problems that older parents and their adult children face but also to look at the variety of spiritual gifts, life experiences, and wisdom that older parents bring to their family, community, and culture.

Each chapter begins with a quote from an older parent that addresses the specific needs facing the situation examined in that chapter. Following that is information about helping to solve the problems facing older parents and other quotes from interviews. Each chapter ends with a Bible quote, a meditation or thought related to spiritual life, and two prayers, one for older parents and one for their adult children. The author's desire is to build understanding and hope for older parents and their adult children.

CHAPTER I

DEPRESSION AND RETIREMENT

I had great plans for my retirement. I have a list of things to do to fix up the house that has been growing longer and longer for the past thirty years. I promised myself that I will spend more time with my children and my grandchildren. I carefully saved to be able to live with a little ease. So why do I feel so rotten? I am depressed and angry. I can't do what I want to do. My children are busy in their own lives and don't have time to spend with me. They say that I should be happy and enjoy my life. They say they would like to be in my shoes. Would they? When I meet people and they ask me what I do, I want to say I am an engineer. Instead, I say I am retired, and I see their faces change. They look at me differently. In a few seconds I seem to go from interesting to useless. My wife says it is all in my mind. It isn't. I was what I did, and now I do nothing, so I am nothing.

—Ralph, 65, retired utilities employee

Ralph is facing postretirement depression, which is common in varying degrees during the first three years immediately following retirement. Once the newness of being retired wears off in the first year, the second year is often the worst for job-loss related depression. In the third year most retirees begin to make the adjustment and come to terms with their new role and

1

position. While his adult children are caught up in their jobs and look at him with envy, Ralph is struggling with loss of identity, self-sufficiency, and self-esteem. Self-esteem is absolutely critical to mental and spiritual well-being. For many people the loss of their job at retirement feels like they have lost the opportunity to make a contribution to society and to their families, especially if self-esteem has been based on what the individual did rather than on who he or she is. In Ralph's case, what he did and who he is are the same.

In the community of faith, though, self-esteem can come from knowing that God's love has prevailed over sin and that victory over hopelessness is a gift of grace. This is not to say Christians do not feel depression and loss of self-esteem at retirement. Rather, Christians have additional resources to help them through the difficult times—the community of faith, their personal relationships with God, the need of Christ for their service in the world.

Ralph's wife perceives her husband's depression as a loss of sense of direction and purpose.

He follows me around the house, wanting to know everything I do and why I do it and offering totally unsolicited advice on how I might do it better. I hope he finds something to do with himself soon or I'll go crazy.

—Janice, 64, Ralph's wife

Ralph's children, on the other hand, think he has the good life now. They see a popular bumper sticker that says "Life Begins When the Children Leave Home and the Dog Dies" as possibly more true than humorous. They are mothers and fathers who work and care for children. They are facing the trials of adolescent children, midlife crisis, and the beginning of menopause. Because their schedules are hectic, they do not see as much of their spouses and children as they wish. So, not working, getting a check each month, and having no children at home sounds like a good arrangement. They are impatient with

Ralph's depression and are critical of their mother for not being more patient with his adjustment. They know Ralph and Janice want them to come by more often, but they just don't have the time. If Ralph Jr. hears one more complaint about lack of attention, he says he is determined to quit speaking to his father for a month.

WORK AND IDENTITY

No one knows better than newly retired men or women how much emphasis is placed in this culture on the connection between the product of one's work or profession and one's identity. Ralph is probably not imagining the reaction of strangers when they learn he is retired. Retirement is seen by many people who are still working as no longer being productive because productivity is often synonymous with work for wages in this society. Some professions have so identified the work with the person that members do not retire until physical health demands it. Usually physicians, lawyers, and clergy are among this group.

In reality, retirement is a change of work or a change of life focus.

I confess that it felt funny at first, not wearing that suit and tie every day. Do you know it took me two whole weeks to decide that I will never, never wear one again? I think the most important part of being retired, though, is that I am not under constant pressure. When I worked I could not afford to be wrong; now I can make a lot of mistakes without fear. I sleep better and feel better than I have in ten years.

—Thomas, 67, retired attorney

Many retired persons report being busier than ever, but not with the same pressures as working for a salary on which one's family depends. Retirement is a change of regimentation. In the working world, most people have hours they work and hours they do not. There is a clear line, and work is valued highly. In the world of retired persons, work and leisure are not as clearly defined. Is the woman who goes to the hospital to rock babies with AIDS working or playing? Is the man who puts in the new flower bed at his house working or playing? Is the grandparent who teaches the grandchildren to fish playing or providing child care?

In this culture the answer often revolves around whether or not money changes hands. If the woman were a nurse's aide and earning an income, she'd be working. If the man were a gardener and earning an income, he'd be working. If the grandparent were at a day-care center earning an income, then child care would be considered work.

Work that does not earn income is seen as leisure, even if in other circumstances it would clearly be called work. In this society, leisure is not as highly valued as work that earns income; therefore, someone who works as a volunteer or without salary is sometimes considered to not really be working.

I have learned to ignore all the little voices that whisper it is time for me to lie down and die. All over the television and magazines people shout, "If you're not young, you're nothing." Well, I'm seventy years old and I am something. The people I love and care for for free in my volunteer work are as important as the ones other people get paid to care for. And if they're important, I'm important.

—Hilda, 70, retired nurse volunteering at local hospice

It can be disheartening to have one's efforts devalued because of a choice to offer them as a gift of love instead of as a service for pay. Churches may not be much different. Unfortunately, the church has sometimes aided this perception by differentiating too much between the work done by lay leaders and professional staff. A retired accountant working as a volunteer treasurer in a small church brings as much professional expertise to the job as the professionals with whom he or she works. A Sunday school teacher with twenty years of experience may know as much about three-year-olds, for example, as the kindergarten teacher down the block. The move to accepting and honoring the work of lay leaders is an important move for the newly retired church member. It says clearly that the community of faith is not drawing a line between paid and unpaid that indicates valuable and nonvaluable.

I have never known a minister to be called of God to a lower paying job. Churches are treated differently if they cannot pay as much, and somehow people think God is into higher pay for higher education or years of experience. I don't believe it. I believe God wants the struggling believers in a small church to have as high a quality of leadership as the biggest church in America. What I make, or even if I'm doing it for free, doesn't make my work for the church lower quality. It's a matter of personal relationship to God, doing what God tells me to do.

—Adele, 71, retired teacher now a lay minister

It is especially disheartening if the devaluation of volunteer work comes from one's own children. The attitude that "Mom is doing a little volunteer work" can be hurtful to a woman who daily risks the pain of grief by loving AIDS babies whom she knows will die.

I take this baby-rocking thing very seriously. I know how to rock babies and I can do this well. My daughter, Andrea, is always trying to get me to skip it and go somewhere or watch her kids for her. "It ain't like you're getting paid for it," she jokes. Really? I get paid more than she'll ever know. I just wish I could tell her how important it is to feel the little ones snuggle up to me and go right to sleep, like they know nothing is going to happen to them when Maggie Lee has them.

—Maggie Lee, 71, retired housekeeper

Maggie Lee's daughter is making a common mistake made by adult children in the years directly following retirement. Andrea assumes that the volunteer work Maggie Lee is doing is just to get her out of the house and keep her occupied. She undervalues the real rewards Maggie Lee gets from her hospital work. Andrea also assumes that Maggie Lee's priorities are the same as hers. In truth, Maggie Lee does not enjoy spending as much time with Andrea's children as Andrea believes. She has always been independent and wants to continue to be independent.

My hospital babies need me a hell of a lot more than Andrea's do. Andrea's children are my own flesh and blood and there isn't anybody who loves them more, but let me tell you they can get to me. When I walk into that baby ward, the nurses say, "Maggie Lee, thank goodness you're here. Little Robby or Little Melinda needs you." Andrea doesn't need me except to save her a little money on the babysitting. She doesn't need me like these babies do.

—Maggie Lee

The three years directly following retirement require the greatest adjustment to change of schedule, work, and priorities. Many retirees are able to make the adjustment in this three-year period. While the level of physical ability and health are important, self-esteem and self-image seem to be more closely linked with the approval of those they love. Even part-time work for pay produces significant differences in perceived health and happiness.

Oddly, both fathers and sons have said that they just wish they knew for sure that the other was proud of them. Fathers, more than mothers, want their sons to be proud of them and of their work. Sons are especially needful of hearing their father's praise. Mothers and daughters share a similar link, but instead of pride in work, it revolves around acceptance and love. The acceptance and approval by adult children of the work or activities chosen in retirement by older parents can be critical to the adjustment of older parents to retirement. Everyone needs such acceptance and praise. No one is too old, too accomplished, too self-sufficient to thrive without it.

PUTTING WORK IN PERSPECTIVE

The importance that this culture puts on work is as old as the first family in the Bible. The Bible doesn't say a lot about what daily activities were like for Eve and her daughters, but it does tell the occupations of Cain and Abel (Genesis 4:2). Their offerings to God were from the fruit of their work. Cain's was unacceptable because God said "sin was lurking" at his door (Genesis 4:7). To this day, though, people often attribute God's displeasure not to the condition of Cain's heart but to the fact that his occupation produced grain and fruit and Abel's produced animals.

Throughout the Scriptures the work people do is lifted up. Lydia wove purple fabric, and the apostle Paul made tents. Peter and Andrew were fishermen. Christ, though, saw these servants of God in terms of their hearts, not their occupations. As a matter of fact, God has often called people to give up their occupations in order to devote their whole attention to matters of the kingdom of heaven. The fishermen became disciples, preaching and teaching. The lesson of the Scripture is that Christians are expected to do all they do as unto the Lord— work, play, leisure (Ephesians 6:7-8).

Older adults are helped to adjust to retirement when they can view this change as a movement from one calling of God—to be a Christian in a specific occupation—to another calling of God. For each older parent the new call might take a different form.

I want the names of women ministers. I am a retired homeland missionary and I want to spend my retirement years in a prayer ministry. My eyes are bad and I am not so good at keeping the children as I used to be. But I can still pray. I can pray and pray and pray. When I pray I feel God's presence and I know that he will never leave me. I thought of all the years I served. It would have been important to know someone was praying for me every day.
—Maria, 67, retired homeland missionary who used to teach reading to children of migrant workers

Not all older adults are called to be prayer partners for others. Some are called to volunteer for child care or to help fix things for others. Some use the same education and skills, but without a salary, for the good of others.

I was upset about leaving the farm. I was depressed and unhappy. Then I planted the largest garden that anyone could imagine and invited everyone in town to come and pick the produce. I loved watching my beautiful vegetables being carried to the tables of all the people in my church and all my friends.
—Rebecca, 75, retired farmer

DEPRESSION

Most older parents adjust to retirement with little difficulty and find their life satisfying after retirement. Others, as in Ralph's case, find retirement a difficult adjustment and react with some degree of depression. Depression in older adults is generally linked to (a) changes in physical well-being; (b) adjustment to a new environment, which may include the loss of independent living; and/or (c) loss of work upon retirement. In some cases depression leads to suicide. A recent national news report said that while older adults represent 13 percent of the population, they account for 20 percent of the suicides.

Saul, the first king of Israel, committed suicide. He fell on his sword so that the enemy would not have the honor of killing him. Although military victory is not the issue, many older adults face circumstances that seem insurmountable. They simply cannot see another way out. Saul's suicide followed a deep depression that came after God made David the new king. His depression resulted in the feeling that God had left him and eventually led him to seek help from spiritualists. Depression can affect one's ability to understand God's message. Sometimes instead of faith changing depression, depression changes faith. Saul could not imagine a time when he wasn't king of Israel and was unprepared for that time when it came.

For many newly retired persons the time is rich and full of happiness. For others they cannot imagine a time when they will not be working. They have not prepared themselves for this drastic change in self-identity and cultural identity.

SPOTTING DEPRESSION

Depression can be characterized by one or more of the following:

1. *A loss of interest in ordinary daily routine.* One signal of this loss of interest is a kind of restlessness that shows itself in the inability to establish a new routine, the loss of concern for hygiene or appearance, unwillingness to participate in home life such as doing household chores, or unwillingness to participate in family activities. People who drop out of church may be suffering from depression. They may find church, with the usual uplifting spirit of the service, too incongruent with their own feelings.

For as long as I have known Ralph he has kept the lawn perfect and watched football every Sunday afternoon. Now when I mention either, he gets quiet and sullen and mumbles, "Who cares?" I tell him I care, very much, and not about the lawn or the football game, but about him. He smiles and rallies for a while to make me happy, but then he slips into his quietness again.

—Janice

2. *Change in sleeping or eating habits.* Sleeping more than usual, especially for long periods of time during the day, is often recognized as depressed behavior. However, depression may be exhibited by manic behavior. Decreased sleep or insomnia can be an indication of depression. Also, eating habits can change during depression. Weight loss and sometimes weight gain are outward indicators. Some people become compulsive eaters and others stop eating altogether. Because food purchasing and preparation patterns change with retirement, some change in eating habits is to be expected. The

office worker who always grabbed a quick sandwich at lunch now has to plan, purchase, and prepare food at lunchtime. This retiree may start skipping lunch altogether, but not because of depression. Likewise, some decrease in sleep is normal as people age. The severity and suddenness of the change of pattern and whether it is accompanied by other depressed behaviors helps determine the severity of the depression and possible need for professional care.

My son is very mad at me because all I eat is ice cream and vitamins. I don't want to cook and I don't want to shop. So I eat ice cream. I sit and look out the window and eat ice cream. I take my vitamins and I eat whole meals when I go out with people. But when I'm home I just eat ice cream.

—Harry, 76, retired house painter

Is Harry depressed or eccentric or does he simply hate to cook? His ice cream habit will make him physically ill, but it may or may not be a signal of depression.

3. *Agitation or slowness.* A marked change in energy and activity can point to depression. Ralph's constant wandering around the house, following Janice, is one example of agitation. Doing the same task over and over again is another example of agitation. Slowness is the cessation of activity and can be seen in the unwillingness to move out of a favorite chair or not wanting to drive to the store. Lethargy is an extreme form of slowness seen in sluggish movements and constant fatigue.

4. *Difficulty concentrating.* There is some natural loss of attention span and concentration with certain illnesses and conditions that may accompany aging. For example, loss of hearing may result in an older parent seeming to not pay attention for long periods of time or to understand all that is said. However, these natural occurrences are not the same as difficulty concentrating as a symptom of depression. In the latter case, the retiree knows that he or she would normally be attentive and aware but cannot seem to focus. All the right environmental

and physical elements are in place, but the person's attention wanders, usually to his or her own problems, feelings, and difficulties.

5. *Feelings of guilt, worthlessness.* For many retirees this is a key problem in the adjustment to not having jobs. Ralph's primary source of depression is his change in attitude about himself related to his work and identity. Other feelings of worthlessness may spring from the inability to do all that one used to do or from the attitudes of family. Adult children who begin to treat their parents as helpless older adults unwittingly foster these feelings of worthlessness. Older parents may also feel guilty about not being able to provide as much income as they believe they should or for real or imagined slights against others.

6. *Recurrent thoughts of death.* It is normal for older adults to think of death more than younger persons because they are closer to death, they have had more experiences of death, and they have a sense of mortality that younger adults do not have. It is normal and natural to think about one's own mortality and about what one wants to leave behind. Knowing about death is different than being preoccupied with it. Christians who are depressed may begin to express doubts about their salvation or talk constantly about heaven and those who have died before them. At the same time, they may need to really work on their relationship to God, and talk of heaven and previous losses is normal as one ages. The answer is in degree.

My mother has bought her burial plot, planned her funeral, and even picked out what she wants to wear. At first this was healthy planning and I was impressed with her wisdom at planning ahead. Lately, it has been really different. I mean she drives by that cemetery once a day and says things like "Don't worry, I'll be gone and out of your way soon." The idea! As if I were counting the days until she dies. It makes me so upset I can't even talk to her. Doesn't she know that I love her and want her with me as long as possible? Doesn't she know how devastated I'll be when she dies?

—Becky, 30, daughter of JoAnna

Yes, JoAnna knows that Becky loves her, but JoAnna has lost her own love of life. It seems to Becky that JoAnna's desire to die is a desire to leave Becky. If JoAnna is suffering from major depression, she may not be able to recover without the help of others.

Harry, the ice cream eater, may be depressed or just may not want to prepare food. At any rate, his son has reason for concern and should ask Harry to get a complete medical evaluation, and a psychiatric one, too, if that is possible. Older adults are often more willing to seek medical care than psychiatric care because of old stigmas and stereotypes associated with psychiatric care. Often older adults who have been active in church may find a pastoral care counselor more acceptable than a psychologist or psychiatrist. Likewise, older parents are more apt to attend workshops, classes, or discussion groups than go for counseling. Harry's son may want to be alert to special classes or seminars in the community and to other ways to get his father out of the house and eating whole meals. Some churches offer a day program for seniors where they are served a hot lunch and have time to spend with other people. Often these programs help two age groups: those who have just retired can work as volunteers in the center, while those nearer the end of their lives may need to come and receive the hot meal.

Besides the kind of major depression described above, psychiatrists generally recognize several different types of depression. For example, a psychotic depression is one in which the older parent experiences hallucinations. The depression discussed here is called an adjustment disorder with a depressed mood and may have one or more of the above symptoms. The symptoms of this kind of depression are linked to a physical or environmental stressor (Blazer 1990, 66-68).

ATTITUDES ABOUT DEPRESSION

Ralph probably would not call what he feels depression. He might say he is having a bad time of it without being clear about his feelings. Many older adults see depression as failure and are embarrassed that they are depressed. Christians may especially experience depression as failure. They may think that if they could just be more faithful, believe more or sin less, they would not feel this depression. Depression is sometimes seen as a failure of faith. This embarrassment may even prevent them from seeking the medical and psychological care they need if the depression becomes severe.

Depression in the second and third year past retirement is common and often works itself out as retirees find new goals and activities. This is the first common occurrence of depression in older adults. The second occurrence may come at any time and is connected with loss of physical ability. The third occurrence may also come at any time and is connected with loss of personal independence. When all three happen at once, as in the case of a person retiring because of a disability and who must accept physical care, the depression can be much more severe.

Some older adults know they need help but will not seek it because they consider psychotherapy or counseling a stigma. Others know something is wrong but do not know what it is.

I don't know what's wrong with me. I've waited for years for the kids to get out of college so we wouldn't need the second income and I could go back to being a plain old ordinary housewife. Now I walk around restlessly. I can't sleep well at all, and I'm tired much of the time. The house is a wreck, and I don't have the energy or desire to take care of it. My pension is so small it's a joke.
—JoAnna, 62, retired secretary

Ralph, JoAnna, and many others in their first years of retirement have to redefine their goals and tasks. Retirement ages are dropping, and as people retire younger, they have more time to be retired. Even though they have been looking forward to retiring and know that leaving the workforce was the right decision, new retirees must make adjustments. They must rediscover their identities apart from their work and must work harder on relationships. Many recent retirees and their spouses have to rediscover one another. The hours formerly taken in work are often spent together.

JoAnna's children tell her they think she is doing just fine and have refused to comment on the cluttered house, which was cleaner when JoAnna was working. They pretend not to notice how much time she spends alone in the house, driving by the cemetery, or her tears, which flow more easily than ever before. Her children talk among themselves about this "phase" mother is going through but do not talk to her about it. Adult children may need to intervene, especially with the help of a pastor, doctor, or family friend, to influence their parents to get professional help.

Both Ralph and JoAnna need to know that they are not alone in postretirement depression. Their children need to know that postretirement depression is common, that it varies greatly in degree, and in a minority of situations can be dangerous. Continuing untreated or unidentified depression can result in suicide or other less dramatic forms of self-destructive behavior. Alcohol and drug abuse, especially prescription drug abuse, often increase in later years. Boredom can turn to drinking, insomnia to dependence on sleeping aids. Older bodies also react differently to alcohol and drugs. The two drinks that used to have no effect on an older adult may cause more severe intoxication as one ages.

LEAVING ONE LIFE FOR ANOTHER

Many older adults love retirement and have planned fulfilling ways to spend their retirement years. Thinking ahead seems to be a key to successful retirement.

I love retirement. I was tired of teaching and now I play golf, bridge, and the piano as much as I want. I'm catching up. I'm making up for all the times I spent in class and school activities when I would rather have been outdoors. I adore my grandchildren and for the first time in many years have real quality time to spend with them and my children. The key for me is to plan my week and be sure to include things I truly love to do. When I first retired I just kind of hung out around the house, and it was boring, frustrating, and unrewarding. Now I have a full calendar and have trouble fitting all the things I want to do into my day.
—Joyce, 67, retired music teacher

Joyce, like many people retiring after years of full-time work, has neglected her own leisure over the years. She sees retirement as a payoff for patience, hard work, and persistence.

I know my neighbors think I'm completely mad. Since I retired, I keep finding things that I don't need to do! You know, you really don't need to rake leaves but once a year. I really don't need to do the flower beds every fall either. I could get used to finding things not to do!
—Allen, 68, retired accountant

LOST DREAMS

One of the realities of retirement is giving up dreams and ambitions that cannot be obtained. Sometimes the physical changes of retirement mean that mountain climbing and camping give way to a mobile camper with a real bed and comfortable chairs. Other times the long-awaited retirement travel just isn't possible.

The first year was great. It was such a relief not to have to be at the office every day at 9:30 A.M.—rain, shine, snow. I felt like I had been released from prison in some ways. Then the new wore off and money got tighter and everyone expected us to travel and do this and that. I had to admit to myself that I hadn't done my job. The money wasn't there and never would be. Europe will still be waiting for me the day I die.

—Ralph

Some older adults find that the loss of dreams and self-esteem is also a loss of their particular ideals and values. This is a major loss and, understandably, depletes the older adult's ability to recover from other losses and adjust to retirement.

Another element of postretirement depression is the loss of work-related opportunity. When one is still in the workforce, one still has the hope of making it big, getting one last promotion, or something similar that would open up a rosier future. Retirement means that there are no more job-related goals and, perhaps more devastating to some people, no more job-related dreams. Much of the character of the American workplace involves some degree of competition. The worker strives to be better, sell more, win more cases, see more patients, be a better teacher, work harder, have better ideas, or whatever. Not only is the money gone, the competition, the sense of winning, and the possibilities of work-related success are also gone.

I have done all I'm going to do in the field of law. I know that my son-in-law, the attorney, will call me now and then and ask advice, but he doesn't really need me. I've done my last big deal and I know it. That feeling of signing the last papers and closing a file is gone forever. I suppose now I'll have to be pleased to birdie now and then in golf. It isn't much.

—Martin, 78, retired corporate attorney

NEEDING TO BE NEEDED

Many retiring persons want to be needed. Many of their adult children think Mom and Dad have it made.

I have always done what I needed to do. I got up every morning and went to work because that is what I had to do. I kept the yard and the house and the car repaired because that was what I needed to do. I did my job as husband and father, and now whenever I try to find out what I need to do, someone says, "Just relax" or "It's your turn to do nothing" or "Whatever you want." I don't know what I need to do.

—John, 63, retired auto salesman

The most volatile relationships seem to be between father and son and between mother and daughter. Because most caregivers are women and most older adults are women, the mother-daughter connection is especially critical. Psychologically, a daughter may feel an intense need to further separate from her mother and form her own identity at the very time in life that her mother needs to become more dependent. The mother perceives the daughter as inattentive and uncaring. The daughter perceives the mother as clinging and controlling.

Because Christians are taught from an early age to honor their parents, the desire to be separate from them, spend less time with them, or not be their primary caregivers can evoke feelings of guilt for adult children. What does it mean to "honor" parents? At least a part of honoring parents is accepting them for who they are and accepting oneself.

When I moved to New York City, everyone asked me how I could desert my aging parents, but that wasn't the way it was. They raised me to follow the call of God, to do my best work, and to live my own life. I honor them by being who I was raised by them to be. And I see that they are cared for, if not by me personally, then by someone I can trust. I see them often. My responsibility is not only for their care but to carry to my children and others the values they taught me. I honor them with each Sunday school class I teach.

—Angela, 34, writer/artist

Angela's parents, then, are faced with a choice—to see their daughter's move as desertion or to see it as the inevitable result of the values taught in a Christian home. How they see themselves may be the deciding factor in their response. The problem of self-concept is intimately linked with the need to be needed. Older adults come from generations who created and built current culture. Rosenberg (1979) described four ways that people develop their self-concept. "(1) Reflected appraisals. People come to view themselves as they are viewed by others. (2) Social comparisons. People judge themselves by comparing themselves to others. (3) Self-attribution. People observe their own behavior and form conclusions about themselves. (4) Psychological centrality. People value particular qualities of themselves."

Older parents, like all people, create their self-image out of this mix. Retirement itself is one way society tells older adults that they are not needed. Then older parents judge themselves by this appraisal. If their adult children join in this appraisal, they feel the judgment more keenly. They may begin to compare themselves with people who are working, and finally, labeling themselves as useless.

Christians will want to add their faith journeys to the combination of self-perceptions that rule their behavior and attitudes. Retirement is a time to think about all God has done in their lives and to begin to work on unfinished business with God. It is not unusual for grief and anger toward God for deaths in earlier decades to come forward again. Often older Christians have had their own parents, as well as other older members of the faith, to give them examples of how to manage the changes of retirement. An elderly beloved minister or deacon can often show the way to those just beginning the retirement journey.

Self-esteem often begins to flourish again as older adults find opportunities to make contributions to society and to give their unique gifts to others.

It used to not seem like much, but I love to make things. I made this little wooden toy chest for my grandson and painted it royal blue with yellow stars. I loved doing it. Then my daughter wanted another for her daughter. I made this one white with a big sunshine on top. Then everyone wanted one. I am going to keep on making them until all my grandchildren have one—all thirteen of them! Maybe when I'm dead and gone, they'll pass them to their children and they'll know their great-grandpa could do something.

—Peter, 74, retired janitor

It is important that older parents know that they have something to offer and that what they have to offer will be remembered. No one outgrows the need to contribute or to have his or her contribution recognized.

MAKING THE ADJUSTMENT

Depression is a common reaction to loss of job to retirement, but it is not, by any means, always a factor. Many older parents are quite able to form deeper and closer relationships with spouses, family, and friends and to fill their time in creative satisfying ways. The retirees that adjust to loss of job the best often have several things in common:

1. *A generally positive outlook on life before retiring.* If people have been bitter and depressed most of their lives, retirement may intensify those feelings. If people have been positive and content most of their lives, retirement will probably not change those attitudes. However, when the positive, content employee becomes a depressed retiree, the depression can be deep and long lasting because the retiree has not previously developed coping skills to deal with depression. Adult children will want to be especially attentive to this group of retirees. Often professional intervention is required.

2. *A good relationship to family, especially spouse.* Retirees who for years have said little to their spouses besides "What's for dinner?" and "Did you remember to lock the front door?" will have greater difficulty learning to communicate in

retirement. Retirees who have continued communication and shared activities will do best. Some couples, and some entire families, have maintained such good relationships that retirement is really a treat for them. They already know how to travel together, how to spend long periods of time together, and how to solve disagreements.

3. *Strong community or organizational ties.* Retirees who belong to churches, synagogues, community action or service groups, or other organizations that stress community and friendship have more support during retirement. Many of these organizations have special activities and programs for retirees, and some are made up entirely of retired persons. Participation brings meaning and purpose, and adult children who try to talk their older parents into "taking it easy" instead of going on outings and activities may not be helping them. An effort that requires energy, even to the point of being tiring, is often satisfying and healthy. People who have regularly been in church have a strong community to depend upon.

4. *Strong parental examples.* Almost all recent retirees can remember their own parents at retirement age. Older adults whose parents are still alive may have special concerns for caring for elderly parents. If parents were able to adjust to retirement, then often their children are able to adjust also. Retirement either strengthens or strains these important bonds.

HOW CHILDREN CAN HELP

Older parents need to know they are respected, loved, and still seen by their adult children as competent, worthwhile persons. Adult children can watch for warning signs of depression and confront parents with their need for help when necessary. Most older adults need what all people going through rapid or intense transition need:

1. *Someone to listen to thoughts and feelings.* Because adult children have become parents themselves in many cases, it is easy for them to slip into the parental mode with their older

parents. Instead of jumping to give advice, though, it is best to stop and listen. Listening to persons' feelings and ideas without judgment or advice validates their maturity and their ability to think for themselves. In listening to older parents, adult children recognize their wisdom. Listening allows older parents, to take their rightful role as the transmitters of traditions, heritage, and knowledge.

2. *Expect them to learn and grow.* The stereotype of retirement as a shutting down of thoughts and work is damaging to egos and spirits. Adult children can help their older parents by expecting them to learn and grow, to continue to have new experiences. Adult children might even suggest a workshop or organization that can aid in creating these experiences through bringing new information into their older parents' lives. An example might be a gift subscription to a magazine about a subject an older adult is interested in exploring.

3. *Bring humor and affection.* Humor and affection are good medicine for every age group. Adult children who bring those into their parents lives help not only their spirits but their bodies.

4. *Be aware of changes or lack of them.* Adult children who are sensitive to changes, both physical and emotional, can avoid some of the most damaging mistakes in relationship to older parents.

5. *Don't group all older adults together.* Personalities, development, and abilities all vary from birth and continue to vary until death. An uncle might have had significant hearing loss, but all older adults do not have the same hearing loss, so talking extra loud can be insulting. Likewise, some older adults are proud of their gray hair; others color it. Think about the individual older parent and act according to that individual's needs.

6. *Confront and argue when needed.* It is patronizing to assume an older parent cannot bear criticism or should be treated as if unable to argue any longer. If adult children see a medical or psychological problem, telling the older adult directly with compassion and affection is best. Adult children

who express themselves both freely and fairly are treating their older parents as intelligent, communicating equals. This gives the older parents the opportunity to express themselves freely and fairly also.

7. *Encourage setting new goals.* One of the best therapies for depression is feeling in control of one's life and having something to look forward to in the future. Important questions for adult children to continue to ask are: What do you want to do? What do you enjoy doing? What would you like to do next year? Adult children often know better than anyone else what brings pleasure and fulfillment to their parents. They can understand this better by asking a simple question: What have I seen bring pleasure and fulfillment to my mother/father in the past? Basic drives are usually consistent throughout life. This may be difficult if older parents are experiencing depression. Also, older adults often resist goal setting because they feel their time is running out. Goals assume a future and are healthy if realistic.

FROM THE SCRIPTURES

Many people find in God a source of relief and release. Perhaps the most vivid and well-known laments of despair are from the Hebrew poetry of the Old Testament, including Job and Psalms. Here is one from the Psalms:

> I am weary with my moaning;
>   every night I flood my bed with tears;
>   I drench my couch with my weeping.
> My eyes waste away because of grief;
>   they grown weak because of my foes.
>
> Depart from me, all you workers of evil,
>   for the LORD has heard the sound of my weeping.
> The LORD has heard my supplication,
>   the LORD accepts my prayer.
>   —Psalm 6:6-9

While the apostle Paul may have learned to be content in whatever situation he found himself (Philippians 4:11-12), most of the Scriptures show people of God who experience the full range of human emotions—depression, anger, grief, sadness, helplessness, joy, peace, contentment, love, fulfillment, repentance, forgiveness.

Becoming trapped in any one of these emotions means a difficult time. The problem is that people of faith have often put an emphasis on the "feel good" emotions and have begun to look at the more unpleasant emotions as a sign of lack of faith or growth. David shows a different picture, as does Job. In the depths of despair or depression, both men maintained their relationship to God. Their feelings were a part of their relationship to God— brought clearly to God—but were not an indicator of the health of their relationship to God. As a matter of fact, Job clearly stood his ground when his friends suggested that it was a secret, unrepented sin that was at the heart of his circumstances.

A Word for the Faithful. Christian older adults need to be encouraged to see their changing circumstances, and the difficulties adjusting to them, as a natural course of life and not a reflection of faith or lack of faith. David's lament in Psalm 6, and others scattered throughout the Psalms, show that depression, despair, and anguish are emotions to be brought to God, not a punishment from God.

A Prayer for Older Adults. Dear God, grant that I may see the changes in my life as opportunities to serve you in new ways. Show me how to bring all that I am feeling and fearing to you and to accept your love in response. Help me not to judge myself or others but to wait upon your mercy; in the name of our Savior. Amen.

A Prayer for Adult Children of Older Parents. Dear God, show me my parent(s) through your eyes and help me to discern when they need me to become more deeply involved in their lives and how to do that graciously and with love. Give them mercy and patience; in the name of our Savior. Amen.

CHAPTER 2

ANXIETY AND CHANGING LIVES

If my daughter drops by with her children one more time this week I am going to say something. I love my daughter, and I adore those children. It's so hard for me to say I can't keep them, but I am tired and they are so loud sometimes. I just can't do all I used to do, and, I don't know why, but the yelling and running bother me. I just want to shout at them to sit down and be quiet. My feet hurt and my head hurts. When I tried to say something last week, my daughter got her feelings hurt and told me her children weren't misbehaving. I didn't mean that they were. They are just being children. Trouble is, I just can't take it like I used to. I worry about yelling at them and about getting nervous and saying something to them. I don't want them to hate me. My daughter and her family are all I have.

—Ellie, 72, retired supermarket cashier

The normal worries and pressures of child care have become too difficult for Ellie. She is growing more and more anxious about her own health and her relationship with her daughter and grandchildren. Her anxiety comes from a common combination of concerns: (1) decreased physical abilities or illness; (2) change in patterns of relationships, such as frequency of visits and amount of time spent with family members; and

(3) change in needs for personal well-being, such as more quiet time. Generalized anxiety can affect anyone and is a part of most major transitions, whatever one's age. However, in a few cases generalized anxiety becomes severe enough for the older parent to need professional care. It can show itself in specific, more severe symptoms.

ANXIETY

Anxiety, often called worrying or nervousness, is a common problem throughout the life cycle. Anxiety may be related to issues of money, health (one's own or someone else's), difficulties within family or community relationships, or a number of other areas of concern. One study found that in a representative community 17 percent of the males and 21 percent of the females over age fifty-five report sufficient anxiety symptoms to be judged candidates for some form of therapeutic help (Himmelfarb and Murrell 1984).

Symptoms of generalized anxiety can be categorized as: (1) hyperactivity, including shortness of breath, sweating, palpitations, and dizziness; (2) motor tension, including trembling or restlessness; and (3) hypervigilance, including feeling keyed up or on edge, having difficulty falling asleep, or being excessively frightened when surprised (Blazer 1990, 110). Several disorders may be symptoms of anxiety.

Panic Disorder. Although it has received a lot of attention in the popular press in recent years, fewer than 1 percent of older adults suffer from panic episodes (Blazer 1990, 111). The anxiety symptoms that accompany panic disorder include dizziness, sweating, feelings of unreality, tingling in the hands and feet, and chest pain.

Obsessive-Compulsive Disorder. This form of anxiety is characterized by obsessions or compulsions that are severe enough to cause distress and interfere with normal life. An example of an obsession would be the fixation of an older parent who cannot let go of an image or idea that a child or grandchild is in danger.

I'm a flight attendant and I love my job. My grandfather has decided that I will die in a plane crash. I have talked and talked to him, but he won't let go of it. He says he lies awake at night imagining my plane going down and if it will burn or explode. It's all he ever talks about to me. I don't even want to visit him anymore because all he does is worry about me. It's ruined my relationship with him because he is constantly after me to quit my job. And I have to admit that sometimes he describes those imaginary plane crashes so well that he scares me a little. I don't want his fear to spill over onto me.

—Mary Ann, 29, granddaughter of Mark

Other older parents develop a compulsive behavior. One woman reports that her mother was changing her clothes eight or nine times a day, every time she felt they might be soiled or imagined they were. A man tells that his father walks around his apartment twenty to thirty times a day checking to see that the windows are locked. He lives on the twentieth floor and is in no danger of an intruder coming through a window.

Obsessive-compulsive disorders are more quickly spotted and are not nearly as common as phobic disorders.

Phobic Disorders. These are the most common disorders affecting people in later life and may be accompanied by anxiety and panic (Blazer 1990, 111). Researchers are not sure why this is so. Older parents may develop agoraphobia, a fear of being in a crowd or a place where they cannot escape easily or without embarrassment. They may begin to confine themselves to home or refuse to travel unaccompanied. Other phobias deal with the physical changes of aging, such as needing a bathroom and not being able to find one or driving in unfamiliar places when one cannot hear horns or sirens easily.

Fear of leaving the house can also come from what some researchers have called vicarious victimization (Waters and Goodman 1990, 39). Because of the rising incidence of violence against older persons, some older adults remember examples of such violence—muggings, purse snatchings, robberies—and feel victimized themselves whenever another older adult is victimized. Their fear is in reaction not to what has happened to them but what has happened to others.

Some phobias may develop slowly and be unnoticed. An older woman may stop driving to the grocery store alone and begin just picking up a few things whenever she can go with someone else or have things delivered. One woman reported living on crackers and milk for two days until a neighbor casually asked if she needed something from the store. It was months before her children knew what was happening. She had accidentally hit another car in the parking lot, and although neither car was damaged, she had been frightened of that parking lot since.

Organic Anxiety Syndrome. Organic anxiety is caused by problems with endocrine function, such as excessive thyroid hormone, low blood sugar, or in rare cases a tumor. Stimulants such as caffeine or withdrawal from depressants also cause organic anxiety (Blazer 1990, 111). Chemical treatment can be effective when anxiety has a biological basis.

Ellie's daughter might do well to ask her mother whether a change in visiting routines would be helpful. For example, would more visits for shorter periods of time be more comfortable for Ellie? Some people find that the length of visits by small children is what produces anxiety. Perhaps it would be helpful to plan outings instead of visits in Ellie's home. If Ellie is anxious about the children running in the house or breaking things, outings would help relieve that anxiety. Ellie might also be suffering from an organic anxiety and need a medical check-up. Her daughter might ask if the anxiety is only in relationship to the grandchildren or if other things seem to be upsetting her as well.

I realize I'm a little bit more irritable. I figure I spent years being patient with my kids. They can be patient with me now. Okay, sometimes I really just want peace and quiet. My daughter-in-law is one of the most perceptive people on earth. She and I talked, and now when I don't want to be disturbed, I turn the rug upside down on the front steps and quit answering the phone. If she drives by and the rug is upside down, she knows I'm fine, just resting my spirit.

—Geri, 76, homemaker

Geri and her daughter-in-law have come to an agreement, and it was based on talking about what they needed.

ANXIETY AND FAITH

Anxiety becomes a part of everyone's life at some time and can have many different causes. Changing lives and circumstances as well as physical/chemical changes can create anxiety. The first day of school causes anxiety for many first graders and their parents. The loss of a job or a family member causes anxiety. A sudden change in income—especially loss of income—causes anxiety. For older parents, changes of routine and income are almost certainly a part of their lives. Worry about the future is at the root of much anxiety. Another anxiety-producing change is a loss of power or control—whether real or feared.

Many older parents have previously lived lives of independence and possibilities. If money was tight, one of the couple may have taken an extra job, or perhaps they economized. However, as the years pass, fewer options are available. In later life the ability to work is limited, and economizing for some may mean choosing between medicine and heat.

Faith offers assurance in times of anxiety. Psalm 34:17-18 speaks to God's assurance of compassion and love for God's people.

When the righteous cry for help, the LORD hears,
    and rescues them from all their troubles.
The LORD is near to the brokenhearted,
    and saves the crushed in spirit.

Many are the afflictions of the righteous,
    but the LORD rescues them from them all.

A part of the question for Christians comes down to faith. Is their faith in their own ability to work or in their own ability to protect themselves? Then loss of these abilities will be quite traumatic. It would be wrong, though, to equate anxiety with loss of faith or lack of depth of faith. Because life is changing, older parents are facing issues that they may never have faced before. Whenever Christians face new challenges, their faith must grow and change.

Christians face all of the same troubles and anxieties that nonbelievers face. The difference is that Christians know that whatever else may happen in their lives—disease, old age, failing sight, changes in finances—the love of God will never leave them. When the Christian community is at it's best in witnessing to God's love, then older members of the community receive extra care and compassion from the community as a whole.

Romans 8:37-39 tells of the extraordinary power of God's love in Christ.

> No, in all these things we are more than conquerors through him who loved us. For I am convinced that neither death, nor life, nor angels, nor rulers, nor things present, nor things to come, nor powers, nor height, nor depth, nor anything else in all creation, will be able to separate us from the love of God in Christ Jesus our Lord.

This familiar Matthew Scripture tells of God's care.

> "Therefore I tell you, do not worry about your life, what you will eat or what you will drink, or about your body, what you will wear. Is not life more than food, and the body more than clothing? Look at the birds of the air; they neither sow nor reap nor gather into barns, and yet your heavenly Father feeds them. Are you not of more value than they? And can any of you by worrying add a single hour to your span of life? And why do you worry about clothing? Consider the lilies of the field, how they grow; they

neither toil nor spin, yet I tell you even Solomon in all his glory was not clothed like one of these. But if God so clothes the grass of the field, which is alive today and tomorrow thrown into the oven, will he not much more clothe you—you of little faith? Therefore do not worry, saying, 'What will we eat?' or 'What will we drink?' or 'What will we wear?' For it is the Gentiles who strive for all these things; and indeed your heavenly Father knows that you need all these things. But strive first for the kingdom of God and his righteousness, and all these things will be given to you as well. So do not worry about tomorrow, for tomorrow will bring worries of its own. Today's trouble is enough for today" (6:25-34).

Worry and anxiety rob older parents of energy and emotional strength. It is different to think about and analyze problems and try to come up with a solution and allow the concerns to take over one's life. Being faithful does not mean being without problems or being without concern about problems. Faith can help keep concerns in a healthy perspective so that they don't become life-ruling anxieties.

I used to lay awake at night listening for every sound after my husband died. I had never lived alone before, and it was a new experience for me. Finally, I just decided that the boogeyman could get me if he wanted to; I just had to get some sleep. I remember waking up and realizing that I was completely okay. Nothing had happened. My pastor was wonderful. He never said, "There, there, dear, God will take care of you." God will always love me and I know God wants good things for me, but lots of good people whom God loves have terrible things happen to them. My pastor said instead, "Try to think about your wonderful family and the life you have had and know that nothing can take that from you."

—Rebecca, 75, retired farmer

ASKING THE RIGHT QUESTIONS

The simplest solution when confronted with anxiety is for children to ask questions in a nonjudgmental way. The goal is information gathering, and whatever answer the older parent gives is going to be helpful in finding solutions. Adult children might preface a questioning conversation by asking permission to intrude. "Can we talk about what is bothering us?" is a good beginning.

1. *What is making you most upset?* Often older parents, like all people, need to verbalize their anxiety to understand it. They may not have even thought through all their feelings and may need the opportunity to put into words their emotional reactions. Some fear and anxiety are normal. If an older woman must drive home through a bad neighborhood, she may be afraid until she reaches home. This is appropriate fear. If she is afraid after she arrives home and is safely inside, then her anxiety may have other sources. If she is afraid of having her home burglarized, this may be an appropriate fear that can be alleviated by better protection. Knowing the exact source of anxiety can help a person to find solutions. Knowing there is no specific source is a signal that a general and chronic distress exists. Medical and psychological care may be needed.

2. *How can I help you be less upset?* Older parents often have specific ideas about what would make them more comfortable.

I don't want anyone breaking into my house while I am asleep. I used to wake up at the slightest sound, but because my bedroom is way in the back of the house and I can't hear so well anymore, I'm afraid I won't wake up if someone breaks in. I keep thinking that someone could be right there in the house and I'd never know. He could walk right up to my bed before I heard him.
—Mary, 86, retired librarian

Mary told her children she wanted an alarm system that would make a loud noise if someone broke into the house. Once installed, the system gave Mary a sense of security because the bell that sounded was so loud she could hear it in her back bedroom.

Other older parents with generalized anxiety are often less focused and may not know what would help. Ellie could not put into words why her grandchildren made her nervous at first, but after thinking about it she told her daughter it was their sudden loud talking and bickering. Her daughter could plan quieter activities for visits and help some, but in the long run Ellie was still anxious. Her anxiety focused on the children when they were there but did not diminish completely when they left. She was suffering some general anxiety. A medical exam showed an increased thyroid function. Ellie was much better after treatment. The impatience that was seen as a character flaw or a failure of faith by Ellie and her daughter was really medically founded.

When children and grandchildren ask what they can do, the answer they are given may be impossible to accomplish. That kind of situation may require negotiation. Mary Ann's grandfather, Mark, would respond to such a question by simply telling her to find another job. Mary Ann is unwilling to make that concession. She might phrase her question differently: "I am not able to quit my job because I enjoy it and I want to go on working. Is there anything besides quitting my job that I can do to help you worry less?" This sets a fair and clear parameter. Children and grandchildren cannot be expected to completely change their lives to help relieve irrational fears in older parents.

If anxiety is chronic and obsessive, there is little that an adult child or grandchild can do. Mark might answer that he wishes she would call him more often to let him know she is all right, or he might ask that she not fly in areas of the world considered to be dangerous. Mary Ann may or may not be willing to do as he asks. Mary Ann and Mark might only be able to agree that they care for one another and will try not to let their disagreement separate them. Even if the outcome is not satisfying to both parties, often the ability to talk about it will help build the relationship. Fears and anxiety increase if not talked through because imagination is often worse than reality.

3. *Have you talked to your doctor about your feelings?* Older parents often see the doctor's role as being solely medical in responding to pain or disease. They may not have considered talking to their doctor about fears or anxieties. They may not have realized that sometimes anxiety can be a symptom of physical illness. They may feel foolish talking to their doctor. Some older parents have said that they do not want to bother their doctor because he is busy or because she has been so good to them that it seems like an unnecessary burden. Older parents may be embarrassed by their anxiety or fears, especially if they see these fears as irrational. Some older persons develop a phobia of their doctor. They believe, irrationally, that if they do not go to a doctor, they will not know they are sick, so they will not be sick. Older women especially complain that they cannot get their husbands to a doctor.

I believe he will have to be unconscious before I can get the medical tests done that I think he needs. I am waiting for him to just be so sick he can't argue—even if it's only the flu—and then I'm going to have the doctor run every test he can think of. I'd rather go through childbirth again than try to get him to the doctor.
—Janice, 64, Ralph's wife

Ralph simply believes that any trip to the doctor results in new medicines and new worries, so he will not go. He claims to have no fear of the doctor. However, his absolute refusal to seek care when he obviously needs it indicates a high level of anxiety, if not about the doctor, then about the physical process of aging and the problems it brings.

There are limits to the amount of help adult children can give when anxiety is generalized. Adult children cannot become counselors and psychologists. The attitude of adult children toward anxiety, though, can help older parents seek other help. The man who was afraid of an intruder twenty stories high did venture to try to talk to his son about it early in the onset of his anxiety. The adult son responded as he would to his ten-year-old and said, "Don't be silly! No one can get in this far up!" The father did not speak of it to his son again but began to become more and more fearful.

Anxiety must be taken seriously, however irrational its focus. A better response might be, "Dad, I can tell you're afraid. Let's talk about what we can do to make you feel safer." Instead of judging the validity of the fear or anxiety, adult children can help older parents talk about the fear. Talking with the children about the fear may help; if not, it is a good rehearsal for beginning to talk about it a professional-care setting.

ENERGY AND TASKS

Many older parents complain that their children believe that since retirement the new retirees have nothing to do. What Ellie's daughter may not realize is that as people age, their ability to cope with small children does change and their energy levels drop. The task that was easy for Ellie at thirty-five is more difficult at fifty-five, hard at sixty-five, and impossible at seventy-five. Ellie's daughter may also be in denial about her mother's aging. She may not want to know the limits of Ellie's abilities now. Everyone understands that the aging process inevitably ends in death, and to admit Ellie is aging is to also admit she is closer to death.

One of the biggest challenges facing older parents in the first years after retirement is learning to communicate their changing limitations without blame, anger, or embarrassment. Their adult children are challenged to have a realistic view of their parents' capabilities and limitations.

These changes in decreased energy levels, loss of hearing and vision, and altered mental capacity are frustrating and hard to face. They are almost inevitable in some degree because they are part of the aging process.

Some physical losses have a greater psychological impact on women, such as loss of fertility and changes in physical appearance. Other losses have a greater impact on men, such as impotence, loss of physical strength, and diminished intellectual acuity.

ROMANCE

Older parents who are no longer married may have a higher level of anxiety because of their feeling of being alone. Adult children may be quick to say, "Of course you're not alone; I'm here." But the reality of life and relationships is that the older parent who feels alone is probably not seeking only companionship, such as their children, grandchildren, and friends can offer. They want romance. Although the frequency of sexual intercourse may lessen as one grows older, adult children do well to not confuse sexual intercourse with romance.

Between the side effects of his blood pressure medicine and the arthritis in my spine, we hadn't had regular sexual intercourse in years. But every night we went to sleep holding hands. We always kissed and touched and hugged. Now I miss that. I miss feeling the warmth of another human being beside me. My son thinks I'm being obscene when I talk about it, but I want a man in my life.

—Alice, 68, retired librarian

Alice is like many widowed or divorced older parents. She has enjoyed a physical relationship of intimacy and support and she does not want to face her remaining years without such a relationship. She knows she cannot replace her recently deceased husband. No one else will ever share the common history, the memories of good and bad times, the knowledge of who she was as a young girl, a young woman, and young mother. Alice is not seeking a replacement for the husband who died but rather a new relationship that will meet specific needs. While some of these needs are physical, some are emotional.

It used to be that when we were together he was the first person I thought of and I knew I was the first person he thought of. As a wife, I had a special place in society. I went to my sister's funeral last week and felt alone. Everyone had a special person to sit with them, to hold them when they cried, and to care for them. Everyone but me. My son and his wife came. They were very close to my sister. He was there for me, but I was second. His wife came first, and she should! I wouldn't want it any other way. I taught my son those priorities! But it doesn't keep me from wanting someone special, too.

—Alice

Alice's son is defensive about Alice going to socials and special events for seniors because she has declared that her intention is to find someone to help fill the void in her life. On a logical, sensible level, he knows he cannot replace his father. He hates to see his mother lonely and hurting and is frustrated that he cannot help. He does not want to feel jealous, but it is what he feels.

There are many more single older women than single older men, and the chances of Alice meeting someone are slim. Even if she does not meet someone, the fun she has had in getting out of her house and doing things is in itself meeting a part of her need for companionship. Some women do not find a physical or romantic relationship with a man but meet another woman with whom they develop a close friendship.

We have coffee every morning and talk last thing each night before we go to sleep. I know it's silly, but I just feel better knowing that someone out there knows what my life is like day to day. I would never have guessed that a friend could mean so much. I mean if I fell and hurt myself, she'd know when I didn't answer the phone to say goodnight, and if I am sick and can't come out for coffee, she knows. I just don't feel so alone. I miss my husband terribly, but I am coping better since I met Julia.

—Robin, 72, retired homemaker

Men seeking a new relationship often fare much better because they have more choices. There is a stereotype of recently widowed men locking their doors, pulling down the shades, and pretending they are not at home when the local widows and divorcees begin dropping by with casseroles and homemade bread. Although it is a stereotype, there is some truth to the image. Women are often more aggressive. There seem to be new rules that guide romance in senior years. Women and men are usually clearer about what they want from a relationship and have no qualms about walking away from someone who does not meet their needs. They have a more realistic picture of what marriage is like and know why they want to be married.

Adult children are wise to encourage new social activities and new relationships. As hard as it is to let go of the image of Mom and Dad together forever, the truth is that some older parents want to be married, and when their first spouse dies or they divorce, a new mate is sought.

Me dating again! It's a little crazy. I married the only woman I ever dated, so every experience is new. I am amazed that I can still blush when a woman looks at me. At my age you'd think I'd be sitting in a rocker. Not me. I'm learning to square dance and I'm taking a cruise. Why I've even been thinking about buying a toupee. And, I'll tell you what. I don't care if my son does think it's silly or if my daughter is worried about some "other woman" living in her mother's house and using her mother's china. They have to adjust. I adjusted to their marriages. I cried in the bathroom for four hours before my daughter's wedding, then I gave her away. It's their turn to adjust.

—Andrew, 76, retired printer

Andrew hit on one of the problems some adult children have with their parents' romances. They feel as if their childhood home has been invaded by someone else. Some even worry about losing their inheritance or having someone else be more important to their parent than they are. Here are some questions adult children might ask about their parents' romances before they become openly critical:

1. *Do I hear my mother/father laugh more?* One of the biggest losses in the death of a spouse is the loss of a shared sense of humor. When tragedy or illness strikes, many older adults have children and friends to help, but when they are feeling good and want to celebrate, they are often alone. Laughter is a great medicine and life lengthener. Adult children will want to be careful about discouraging someone who brings laughter into a lonely parent's life. However, if the older parent seems to be more depressed, anxious, or worried than before, then the relationship may not be helping. Often the problem is that older parents are as unwilling to accept advice on romance as their adult children once were. The best advice is to let older parents make mistakes in relationships, to be hurt and try again, just as they allowed their children to do when they were dating.

2. *Is my mother/father going out more?* Sitting home because of depression or anxiety is unhealthy and can make the depression and anxiety worse. Social activities and new adventures are important at any age. Sometimes the going out is more important than the who with. If the date is not Mr. or Ms. Perfect, remember that older parents are looking for much different things at age seventy than they were at age seventeen. This is not a sixty-year commitment.

3. *Is it hard for me to watch my mother/father in a new romance because I am still grieving?* Grief moves at different speeds. What is too soon for some is just right for others. Older parents cannot be expected to continue to grieve until all of their children are through the process. Everyone needs a period of mourning, and jumping into a new relationship too soon can make that mourning more difficult. Older parents, likewise, cannot expect their children to be ready for a new stepmother or stepfather at the same time they are ready for a new relationship. Understanding and patience are needed all around.

BEING ONESELF

To accept the physical changes and limitations of aging, older parents need to be reminded by their adult children of what they offer to the family. The unique history, personality, and character of every older parent is a particular gift to the family, even if his or her physical and intellectual abilities have changed.

In all close associations, frequently the things that make a person unique also have the quickest ability to irritate others. As older parents age, some of their habits and attitudes may be emphasized. The mother who always told long, involved stories may tell them more often, the same ones over and over again, and be less attentive to when she is boring others. The father who always fixed his own car may insist on continuing to fix it after his ability to do so has diminished.

The challenge to adult children is to let go of their desire for their parents to be anyone other than exactly who they are. All mentally healthy people continue to learn and grow, and that is a clear goal of any age. However, the ability of older parents to change significantly is sometimes limited. The father who has always had an annoying habit of pointing when he talks will most likely continue to do so. That same father, though, may be learning about dealing with grief and could share that learning with his adult children, pointing as he did it.

ROLE CHANGES

Older parents may go through several role changes during this stage of their lives. In all likelihood their parents are deceased and they have already had to cease thinking of themselves as someone's son or daughter. Many of their friends and siblings have also died. Each close death has an impact on the older adult.

Widowhood. Over two-thirds of the women in this country are either widows now or will become widows (Blazer 1990, 226). The death of a spouse robs older persons of the most intimate and supportive relationship they have had for most of their lives. There are exceptions, when marriages were unpleasant and death is actually a relief. Even in these extreme instances, widowhood requires adjustment.

Social life changes. Many events that were organized around couples exclude widows and widowers, and some friends even feel uncomfortable with a single woman or single man. Widows and widowers often join together and form their own social groups. These supportive communities do have a drawback; they lack intimacy with both genders. Long after sexual intercourse has ceased, older adults need physical intimacy and physical touch. Family life changes. Often adult children step up their communication with and "watching over" of widowed parents. This can be a mixed blessing.

My daughter calls me every day to see if I took my heart pill. I forgot the day my husband was buried and she was there. So now she thinks she has to remind me. I've taken that pill for years without her. I know it's because she loves me and she knows I forget things, but does she have to make it worse than it is? I may forget milk at the market and to mail a birthday card, but I don't forget my pills . . . yet.

—Libby, 71, retired cook

At the same time, Libby's daughter, Sally, has reason to be concerned. The period of intense grief following the death of a spouse can be marked by forgetfulness. How can Sally find the balance in this new role of watch care? When both parents were alive, Sally was able to be less concerned because she assumed they would care for each other. Now she assumes she must try to fill her father's role. Of course she cannot. The essence of this grief is that Libby, and other older parents who are widowed, have lost what can never be replaced. Romantic love seems to them to be something for younger people, and many feel their destiny is to complete their lives alone.

The adjustment required in this period is to discover how to be alone, but not lonely. The need for physical and emotional intimacy is great at any age. Recently widowed older adults need touching, cuddling, hugging, and other forms of physical closeness. Adult children may find that the distant parent who never hugged much becomes a hugger. Older parents may choose to get a pet or to take dancing lessons. The need for compassionate physical touch spans all of life and is particularly strong following the death of a spouse. Adult children who know their parents' value system and habits might be able to help them find ways to get their needs for physical touch met.

Men sometimes have more difficulty adjusting to widowhood than do women. Partially this is because most men expect to die before their wives and perhaps because in traditional marriages of sixty years ago the women took care of most of the men's daily household needs. The norm is that women live longer. Men are often surprised when they are left alone. Some men do not develop close friendships outside of their marriage.

Off-time events. Throughout their lives older parents have seen a certain order to life. They marry. They have children. Their children marry. Their children have children. They grow old. They die. Their children grow old. Their children die. Older adults have a set of expectations about how life will progress. When this set of expectations is not met, adjustments must be made.

Perhaps the most traumatic event any person faces is the death of a child. It is a shock to the natural order of life and often poses a bigger problem for older parents than the death of a spouse. The other children may experience several reactions from their parents. The parents may become overly attentive or overly possessive of the remaining children. They may focus so intently on their loss that the surviving children feel left out and isolated. In extreme cases they may become self-destructive or give up on living.

Everyone wants to know why I won't eat. I won't eat because I want to die. That isn't so hard to understand. Did you notice the date on my (hospital) chart about when I quit eating. I quit eating on December 20. It was the first anniversary of my daughter's death. I wonder how long it will take me to be with her.
— Andrew, 81, retired salesman and patient in
hospital intensive care unit

Andrew died a week after this interview. The most the staff could get him to eat was a little custard. He felt cheated that his daughter died first and so fought back the only way he knew how. Failure to eat is a common weapon used by older adults to try to gain control in their lives. They cannot run away or move. They cannot seek a new job or other change. But they can refuse to eat, which may be seen by them as their only real power.

Children who are more ill than their parents is another out-of-time event. Some older parents have to care for adult children, and this prevents them from slowing down their own activities and from being cared for themselves.

Absence of grandchildren is another stressful family circumstance. Most older parents expect to be grandparents and miss out on a significant cultural identity when they are not. Sometimes older parents mourn what did not happen and must find new ways to identify themselves in the society.

I can't do much, but I do what I can. I used to climb mountains, now I look at them. I used to have big dreams, too. Now I just nap a lot and have good dreams. I feel like I am leaving a lot of things undone. I look at my little grandchildren though and I figure what I didn't do they can do. I hope that is enough.
— Martin, 83, retired railroad engineer

Martin has reached a healthy point in life. Like many older parents, he knows the limits of what he can do but sees that he is not alone in the world. His family can also claim successes, and he feels he is a part of all they do. Older parents who are able to understand that although their contributions have changed they are still important have a happier later life.

FAMILY ROLES

Family roles shift for older parents, especially when there is a shift in the family composition through the death of either a parent or child. If the person who was always the joker has died, someone will need to fill that role. If the person who always organized the family gatherings is gone, someone else will have to do that chore.

Some common family roles are facilitator, victim, manager, caregiver, and scapegoat. The loss of one of these results in a shifting of family roles, and sometimes, in what seems like a blink of an eye, the person who always was a victim may become a caregiver. The family system shifts to take care of its needs almost without the family member realizing what is happening. There can be conflicts when a new role thrust upon a family member is uncomfortable.

Mothers and daughters. One myth of later life is that the roles of mother and daughter are always reversed, with the daughter becoming the mother's caretaker and the mother dependent upon her daughter. Another myth of the aging process is that the mother would not age as fast if the daughter paid more attention to her (Brody and Semel 1993, 32). The reality is that the aging process can be slowed by lifestyles that are healthy and helped to be less difficult to bear by medical care. Everyone, without exception, grows older. Guilt and frustration are set up by a mother's desire to have attention and the daughter's helplessness to stop the infirmities of age.

As mothers deal with their fears of abandonment by their daughters, the daughters may be struggling with a fear of becoming like their mothers and of growing older themselves. These daughters often love and appreciate their mothers, admiring them a great deal. However, they want their own identity, and the close tie with their mothers during the aging process makes them feel less separated and calls into question some of their independence.

Fathers and sons. To a lesser extent, because sons are less often caregivers and the majority of older parents are women, fathers and sons face some of the same realities. Fathers often define their success as parents and as humans by the kind of sons they have raised. More so than with daughters, sons feel a pressure to make sure that Dad is proud of them. Men, both fathers and sons, may have a sense that they should be in control, therefore their wills clash and neither can give way.

Usually sons have less experience at caregiving. Often they want the care of their elderly parents to be taken on by their wives or daughters. Father may be better cared for by his daughter-in-law, but she will never make up for the perceived neglect of his son.

The myth that in-laws are difficult to deal with has made some older adults doubt that they will be cared for if a daughter-in-law or son-in-law is the one who is left. This isn't true.

I loved my mother-in-law and would have done anything to care for her. She knew the son she had raised was just like the man she had married, and she knew better than anyone what I needed to do to help make my marriage work. I would not have made it without her. It was a privilege to care for her when she was old. I know my own daughter-in-law will care for me if my son cannot. I have no fear of being old, just a desire to postpone it.

—Rebecca

Another myth about the care for older persons in this country is that somehow older parents are neglected. Many times, no matter how much adult children try to do, it does not seem to be enough, because they cannot do the impossible—make their parents younger, healthier, and happier. Older parents normally understand that their children cannot make up for all the losses in their lives, but they still feel the pain of their losses. Their adult children may realize that they are doing a lot for their parents but still recognize their parents' losses.

GAINING WISDOM

Older parents who are able to make the adjustments in family roles and become accustomed to their own changing abilities can offer their adult children the gift of wisdom.

1. *Maintaining humor.* The best medicine for most agonies is laughter and genuine affection. Humor that laughs at life, but not at people, is healthiest.

I remember my father making use of his false teeth by chasing the grandchildren around the room with them in his hands, pretending to bite them. I never thought it bothered him to have false teeth, only that he chose to make it into a game instead of an omen of old age. He loved to laugh and was making jokes until he died.
—Rosemary, 49, daughter of Libby and her late husband, Jack

2. *Keeping the heritage.* The family's history is retained in the collective memory of all of its members. Often the older members of the family have the role and responsibility to pass on their share of the collective memory. Carrying out this role can provide a significant boost in self-esteem when the family receives this gift. An even more important boost in self-esteem can come when the family members seek out this gift and use tape recordings, diaries, or other means to preserve it for generations still unborn.

3. *Speaking up.* Older parents who learn to say what they need and want, even if their needs and wants are not all met, adjust better to changing roles than those who keep silent.

4. *Recognizing wisdom.* One of the areas where all parents and children sometime quarrel is over the issue of advice giving. With age comes a natural collection of information and knowledge. Perhaps wisdom can be defined as knowing when, where, and how to share knowledge. Older parents could often use lessons in tact in giving advice, but it is also important for adult children to realize that it costs very little to listen to advice, solicited or unsolicited.

All of these suggestions work best when older parents are healthy and mentally cogent. Sickness can change relationships in an instant. The next chapter deals with illness.

A Word for the Faithful. Anxiety becomes a problem when limited energy is used to worry about circumstances or problems that the worry cannot change. Anxiety robs older parents, and their children, of health and peace of mind. Faith, while not a quick fix for problems, enables believers to understand that there are some gifts from God—life, love, peace, and hope—that can't be touched by the circumstances and events of the world.

A Prayer for Older Parents. Dear Lord, my world is changing and I am worried about what will happen to me and those I love. Give me peace of mind and clear direction on what I need to do. Give me the courage to talk to those who love me about what is worrying me, and give them the understanding to help me through this time. Amen.

A Prayer for Adult Children of Older Parents. Dear God, help me not to be impatient with my parents and their concerns. Remind me that all of us face changes and that they have real concerns and fears that may be overwhelming. Lead me to ask the right questions and respond in an understanding way. Amen.

CHAPTER 3

MEDICAL QUESTIONS AND NEEDS

My body has become an adventure in medical care. Every week, it seems, I have a new ache or pain. I take so much medicine and I still don't feel good all the time. I sometimes think I should just flush it all down the toilet. It costs too much and I feel lousy anyway. My daughter treats me like I'm an invalid already. She calls to see if I've taken my pills and insists on going to the doctor with me. I tell her I'm just old. Old is old; no pill will change it. And she talks about me to the doctor as if I'm not there. Then she says to me, "Did you understand?" I understand a lot. I know I will never be well again. I know that I lie awake at night and wonder if I will die of cancer or heart disease.

—Mary, 80, retired nurse's aide

Without exception, older parents experience some form of illness or condition that limits the activities they once found easy. The degree of limitation and seriousness of the illness varies greatly. Some are unique to the individual; some are common in various degrees to almost all older adults. The onset of these common problems is seen as a mark of aging, a rite of passage of sorts. One woman described these illnesses as road signs on the journey to death. These same illnesses can also create a certain camaraderie among older parents. Knowing they are not alone in these adjustments can make the illnesses bearable. They become members of what one man called the "club of can't"—can't see as well, can't hear as well, can't walk as well, can't eat as well.

COMMON PROBLEMS

Not all older persons experience the onset of expected medical problems, such as loss of sight, hearing, memory, and mobility at the same rate. Most older parents resent being treated as if they are more physically impaired than they are. They cling to every bit of health and well-being that they have. On the other hand, some adult children fail to understand that their parents are truly impaired and have difficulty dealing with expectations they cannot meet. In a family with several adult children, there may be differing opinions about the need older parents have for care. They may find medical questions particularly troubling: How sick are my parents? What should I do to help them? How much help is enough? How much supervision of their care is appropriate? Do I need to go to the doctor with them?

Most older adults are not seriously ill, nor do they experience significant disability until the last stages of life. However, the physical illnesses or impairments they do experience can have a devastating emotional effect. Older parents tend to see the onset of certain common ailments, such as loss of hearing and vision, as omens that worse disease and even death are on the way. In fact, chronic physical illness begins long before retirement. As many as 72 percent of persons between the ages of forty-five and sixty-four suffer at least one chronic physical illness. Over the age of sixty-five, 80 percent suffer some illness and 50 percent suffer more than one (Blazer 1990, 182). Adult children may be seeing in themselves the beginnings of the same illnesses that are acute in their parents.

I have arthritis in my knee, just enough to hurt with changes of the weather and to make coming down the stairs uncomfortable. My mother can't get out of a wheelchair now. Her knees are swollen and she is in constant pain no matter how much medicine they give her. I haven't told her that my knee hurts. It seems like such a little thing compared to hers. I look at her and see myself in twenty-five years. It kind of makes me angry. It's not fair to have to know. I dread being old. I wish I didn't know what was waiting for me.

—Peggy, 51, daughter of Elizabeth, 78

Most common illnesses in older parents are not life threatening, but they interfere with social and physical functioning to differing extents and are constant reminders of the passage of time. Physical illness has long been recognized as a major cause of emotional problems in later life. The loss of control over one's physical body can be a source of major stress.

Some of the first complaints of most older persons have to do with loss of hearing, changing sleeping and eating habits, failing vision, and limited mobility. Vision begins to deteriorate in the late thirties and early forties, and by the time retirement comes, most people are wearing some form of glasses. Glaucoma is another early problem, with cataracts developing in the late sixties and seventies. There are, of course, some older adults who maintain good vision until very late in life, but they are a minority. Loss of vision that affects the ability to work, read, and drive can also be emotionally difficult. Many people realize this, so early eye care is common among most older adults. Some do not realize the amount of improvement that surgery such as cataract removal and correcting nearsightedness can offer and may need to be encouraged to consider a surgical option.

Some hearing loss can be expected by most older adults, but severe loss is not usually an issue until after age seventy. While hearing aids can offer some help, a total improvement for this kind of hearing loss is not possible at this time. Hearing aids carry a social stigma in the minds of some older persons. There are also other problems with many hearing aids. They can be less effective in restaurants because of background noise or may produce a high-pitched squeak. Many older adults welcome any help they can find to understand and communicate. Others refuse hearing assistance and become isolated, even among people.

My father wouldn't admit he needed a hearing aid. He just made us all shout. Mother finally bought one and then complained that we were always too loud. I live far from my family, so most of our conversations were by phone, with Dad on one extension telling me to speak up and Mom on the other telling me not to yell. I finally licked the problem with modern technology. I bought phones with adjustable volume. Dad turns his way up and Mom keeps hers on normal and I speak as I always did. What a difference technology can make!

—Wally, 45, son of William

When older parents cannot see or hear well, they are socially impaired. They are unable to read road signs and often cannot drive in unfamiliar places. They have trouble reading a hymnal or songbook or participating in meetings or committees where reading is required. Hearing loss makes communication difficult and is sometimes embarrassing when relatives must speak loudly or almost shout in public places. Older parents may choose to spend less time at social events outside their house, becoming more reclusive. While this may not be the best way to handle these difficulties, it may be the only way older parents know to deal with the problem. Adult children can be observant about changes in social habits and try to help older parents remain active.

Insomnia, the inability to sleep, increases proportionately with age. In a survey, nearly 50 percent of persons over the age of eighty complained of sleeping problems. In looking at these problems, it was discovered that 15 percent of persons over the age of sixty-five slept fewer than five hours a night, with sleep complaints reported twice as frequently among females compared to males (Blazer 1990, 143).

Eating habits may also change. Many people find they desire less food in later years, and some become nibblers instead of eaters. Also, trouble with digestion means a limit on certain kinds of food. Loss of sleep and nutrition can contribute not only to a decline in physical health but also to a change of attitude, depression, and fatigue.

I don't eat much anymore. I still like the same things, just less of them. I'm losing weight and the doctor is a little worried, but I just don't want to eat. Can your body just decide to quit? Maybe this old body knows it's time to quit eating and get ready to die. My daughter hates it when I talk like that. I think it's pretty normal for someone my age to know the time is coming. My body knows and its telling me.

—Elizabeth, 78, retired attorney

Elizabeth is right about her body beginning to shut down. Less food and less sleep are natural signals that less activity is needed. Sometimes, though, these natural decreases in eating and sleeping come too rapidly for the body and the mind to keep up with them. Without enough food or sleep, Elizabeth, and other older adults like her, will experience loss of energy and fatigue. Her daughter is faced with spending time coaxing her mother to eat and trying to get her to take sleep-inducing medication or watching her mother's energy decline and patiently deal with her mother's increased irritability.

Many older parents dislike the idea of additional medication. If there are hints of self-destructive behavior, adult children are reluctant to have sleep-inducing medication in their parents' grasp.

Mobility is another limiting factor that begins to develop in the forties and then progresses. Arthritis is perhaps the most common joint problem. Bone deterioration, especially osteoporosis in women, can present a variety of difficulties, and hip and knee replacements have become more and more common. The use of a cane is a symbol of aging. When used properly, a cane can prevent falls and other injuries and help lengthen the time older persons can be mobile. Many older parents begin to fear falling because they have seen that serious hip injuries often mark the end of independent living. The ability to get around one's own home is a high priority for older adults. While those with vision or hearing problems can often adjust to living alone in their own familiar homes, older parents with mobility problems, especially those that are serious enough to confine them to a wheelchair or a bed, cannot.

Loss of memory is another problem that severely limits independent living. Most short-term memory loss can be easily dealt with if older parents are willing to admit to their problem. Alzheimer's disease is the most common type of senile dementia in Western society. As many as 15 percent of those persons over the age of sixty-five may suffer at early symptoms of the disease and as many as 30 percent of persons over eighty years of age may be affected (Blazer 1990, 36). Perhaps no other disease is as dreaded by older parents as Alzheimer's. While progress is being made in the treatment of this disease, there is currently no cure nor is there a treatment that seriously impedes its progress.

I can't remember things like I used to. My daughter teases me that my memory has always been bad and I shouldn't worry about it, but I know it's worse. I just don't know how bad it will get. I know my older sister doesn't even know her name anymore. I wonder if my memory loss is just normal getting-older stuff or if I have the same disease (Alzheimer's). I wake up each day glad that I know who I am, waiting to see if this will be the day that I forget something so important that there will be no question. I want to die before I don't know who I am.

—Hilda, age 82, retired bookkeeper

In addition to memory loss, Alzheimer's symptoms include loss of communication skills, loss of attention, perceptual problems, angry emotional outbursts, increased levels of suspicion, and, in the early stages of the disease, moderate to severe depression. The difference between normal memory loss and Alzheimer's has been described in terms of awareness. The average older adult forgets, remembers what has been forgotten, then forgets that it was forgotten. The Alzheimer patient forgets, forgets that something is forgotten, and doesn't care that it is forgotten (Blazer 1990, 36). In other words, Hilda, because she is aware of her forgetfulness and because she eventually remembers what she has forgotten, is probably not exhibiting symptoms of early Alzheimer's disease.

Besides these common losses of memory, hearing, vision, mobility, appetite, and sleep, there are other diseases that are common and often the cause of death for older parents. These are, of course, cardiovascular heart disease and cancer.

Men and women both must be concerned about heart disease. For women this concern develops ten to twenty years after menopause when their estrogen production ceases to protect their hearts. For men this concern can begin as early as fifty and last until death. While diet and exercise can certainly help ward off heart disease, heredity is still a major factor. Heart disease is one of the two major causes of death for older adults; the other is cancer.

Certain cancers develop more often in later life. Many men develop prostate cancer, which is detectable now by a blood test and curable in most cases. Women develop breast cancer more after the age of fifty, so early detection can mean a significant difference in survival. Colon cancer is also more prevalent in later years in both men and women, and early detection is important.

Most people are afraid of cancer. The word itself conjures up images of a long, lingering, painful death. This is because twenty years ago few cancers could be treated and cured. Now almost 67 percent of all cancers can be treated and cured if found early enough. The emotional impact of a cancer diagnosis does not end with the older patient. Often adult children will see the diagnosis of cancer as certain death for their parents and an omen about their own future. They begin to deal with a grief process around the loss of their parents before that loss is certain.

Heart disease has a similar emotional impact, although most people are familiar with the range of successful treatments available. Adult children might not be aware of the psychological trauma open-heart surgery can have on their older parent, and many are surprised by the profound effect such surgery can have on the emotions of older adults. Personality changes are not unusual.

I cry now almost all the time. I think of my children when they were babies and I cry. I think of my grandchildren and I cry. I never used to cry. I guess I have a lifetime of tears inside and they're finally coming out.

— John, 76, retired school bus driver

For some families the personality changes are not hard to accept. John had prided himself on being completely nonemotional. His wife said she had only seen him cry on two occasions, and his children had always wondered if he really loved them. While they know he is crying too much, the new softness and vulnerability have allowed them to talk with him in ways they never experienced before. Other changes are not so easy to accept.

I can't believe how demanding he (my husband) has become. He used to be the most easy-going man you would ever meet. Now everything has to be his way. He'll say to me, "I almost died. I'm going to die soon. A dying man should get what he wants." The doctor says he has another five to ten years since the surgery. Not if he doesn't straighten out and act right. I may have to kill him with my bare hands.

— Sally, 73, homemaker

Sally would never seriously consider murdering her husband, but her frustration level is reaching the breaking point. Their children, though to a lesser degree because they do not live with him, feel the same tension. John has dipped into savings to buy a fancy car, a new television, and a whole collection of different types of gadgets. John's brush with death has made him self-indulgent and perhaps inconsiderate.

For some patients heart surgery results in hallucinations and deep psychosis.

I saw the devil sitting on the heart monitor keeping time with my heartbeat. I felt he was keeping me alive and I had to watch him every minute. If I took my eyes off him for a moment, he would shut my heart off. I tried to stay awake all night to watch him. I dozed off once and woke up so frightened I couldn't believe I was still alive. Finally, a nurse came in and I told her. She told me she would take care of it and blocked the monitor from view, and when she moved, the devil was gone. She moved the monitor so I can't see it though, and now I won't know I'm dying until my heart completely stops. I know this sounds silly, but it was very real to me, very real.

—William, 74, retired police officer

The most severe symptoms of psychosis and hallucinations often disappear after patients leave the intensive care unit and are on a more regular routine. However, adult children might expect some personality changes in their older parents following open heart surgery. Adjustments can be hard for both parents and children.

Strokes are also common in older adults. As with other diseases that limit mobility and communication, strokes can severely limit older adults' ability to live independently. Strokes have a wide range of severity and may result in symptoms as minor as difficulty in moving certain muscles or as radical as paralysis or coma. Strokes are blood vessel incidents that affect the brain and produce difficulty in muscle coordination and communication.

UNUSUAL PROBLEMS

Alcohol and drug abuse, hypochondria, and medical misdiagnosis are special medical problems that involve a minority of older persons, but when present they can create large problems.

Alcohol and Drug Abuse. Older adults have less body water, less extracellular fluid, and a higher percentage of body fat. This means that their tolerance for alcohol is not the same as when they were younger. Therefore, the same amount of alcohol will result in a higher intoxication level in older adults. Alcohol is also used by some older parents to help them sleep or to mask feelings of depression or anxiety they may be experiencing. The same is true for drugs, mostly prescription drugs, to which they have become addicted or use inappropriately. A good physical, an honest health evaluation, and perhaps an evaluation by a mental health professional can help pinpoint the source of the alcohol or drug problem. Sometimes older parents simply need to understand that the physiology of drinking changes as they grow older.

Older parents must be aware of the increased risk of using alcohol. Sometimes people who have drunk moderately all of their lives must be encouraged to drink less or give up drinking altogether. Adult children may find this encouragement to be a difficult task. As with most substance abuse issues, clear, direct communication from more than one person about their observance of the problem is the best approach. Combined with the advice and support of a group such as Alcoholics Anonymous, the problems are not insurmountable.

Hypochondria. Because older parents often have a variety of legitimate symptoms and complaints, their adult children may have difficulty in deciding if there is a deeper problem of hypochondria. Only an intense medical history by a physician or psychotherapist can really make that determination. Often hypochondriacs go from doctor to doctor, "shopping" for one who will give them the treatment or medication they want. This makes a diagnosis of hypochondria doubly difficult, because no one physician has the entire picture of the older parent's health.

Adult children can encourage their parents to have records forwarded from one physician to another and can ask to go with their parents to see new doctors. Older parents should also be encouraged to take all of their medicine to a new physician so he or she knows about everything they are currently taking. Some medicines are dangerous when mixed, and the hypochondriac may not tell the heart specialist about all the medicine the kidney specialist prescribed.

Often hypochondria is not new to the older parent but an intensification of an already existing problem. If this is so, the adult children may be well prepared to help their parents.

I just gather all the medicines together and get my calendar where I write all the doctors' names and information and go with Mom wherever she goes. I'm her personal medical secretary. Often the doctor sees me at first as an interfering child and may even hint that I am overprotective. As treatment progresses the doctor understands. Mom gets upset because she can't get medicine for the latest illness, usually one she read about in a women's magazine, and we start the whole process over with someone else. I wish we lived in a little town so there would only be two doctors to choose from and they'd both know her. In this city it'll be years before we run out of doctors. I'll run out of room for the prescriptions in my bag first.
—Allison, 32, daughter of Helen, 65

While Allison's way of coping is not easy, she is allowed to help. Many hypochondriacs will not allow their children to talk to their physicians, so children face the difficult choice of whether to go behind their parent's back or not know if the care being received by their parent is appropriate.

Misdiagnosis. In this age of increasing medical knowledge and specialties, many physicians concentrate their efforts in healing older persons. However, not all older persons have such specialists available. It is possible for health-care professionals to see problems that look like the normal aging process and fail to recognize them as symptoms of a curable or treatable disease. A popular television show recently focused on a beloved older doctor whose shaking hands made it impossible for him to steadily hold a scalpel. This television character had decided in his own mind that it was his age at fault. A younger doctor discovered instead a treatable disease that allowed the older doctor to continue to operate. This fiction is too close to fact for some older persons. They assume their symptoms are a part of the aging process, and so they do not even report them to their doctors. Many of the symptoms of aging can be treated, if not cured.

I thought I was just old. I was tired all the time and couldn't concentrate. I didn't heal as quickly and had shaky spells where I felt really weak. I remembered my dad used to say, "Old age ain't for sissies," and I thought, Boy I must be a real sissy. Then my doctor did a sugar test and discovered I have diabetes. A pill a day and change in diet—and presto, I feel fine. Should have told him months ago.

—James, 69, gardener

Even though older adults may have a favorite physician and are reluctant to go somewhere else, most doctors encourage second opinions and many will even recommend another doctor for the second opinion. Older parents should be encouraged to report all symptoms, even those that they think are "just old age." Adult children can urge their parents to seek second opinions and schedule additional visits to the doctor when appropriate.

Some doctors do not listen carefully to older adults' descriptions of their symptoms because they assume that age is the major contributing factor. But not every condition has to do with age, and people of the same chronological age may have very different levels of illness. Adult children may want to be sure that health-care professionals are treating their older parents as individuals.

FAITH AND ILLNESS

The Scriptures are full of stories of people who are sick and are healed by divine intervention or by their own faith, as Jesus often said. This raises a troubling question for some older parents: Why can't I be healed? They wonder if it is a matter of their lack of faith or if God wants them to be sick. Each illness is different. Every person has different spiritual strengths and needs and is able to cope with illness in a variety of ways. Job is perhaps the most troubling vision of illness in all the Scriptures. As his body was covered with boils and sores, he could get no relief from the pain. He scraped his sores with a pottery shard and cried out to God.

There was an intervening time of suffering before God answered. God's answer was that God is God and Job was not God and had no right to question what happened in his life. An important part of the prayers and songs of the psalmist is recognition that God's power and presence is the basis of all life.

> I will bless the LORD at all times;
>> his praise shall continually be in my mouth.
> My soul makes its boast in the LORD;
>> let the humble hear and be glad.
> O magnify the LORD with me,
>> and let us exalt his name together.
>
> I sought the LORD, and he answered me,
>> and delivered me from all my fears.
> Look to him, and be radiant;
>> so your faces shall never be ashamed.
> This poor soul cried, and was heard by the LORD,
>> and was saved from every trouble.
> The angel of the LORD encamps
>> around those who fear him, and delivers them.
> O taste and see that the LORD is good;
>> happy are those who take refuge in him.
>> —Psalm 34:1-8

To understand illness, believers must begin with the lesson Job learned: God is God. Add to that the lesson of the psalm: The Lord encamps around those who have reverence for him. This is not a promise of wholeness in the sense of the end of physical illness but a promise of wholeness in the sense that in the middle of the struggles of illness the people of faith are not alone and are under the power of God. Wholeness is not the absence of illness but the presence of faith. If the faith community can cling to that knowledge, then the mercy, grace, and healing of God through Christ become possible. Mercy and grace are always with those who believe. Healing has it's own timing and sometimes a different form than one might expect. The ultimate healing is death, when the spirit goes home to God, and it is toward this ultimate healing that all people journey. The older members of the community of faith are often acutely aware that they are closer to the end of that journey. In eternal life there is no longer pain, or even the possibility of pain, and all infirmity is gone.

I learned to be very careful about praying for healing for my elderly, very sick parishioners without talking to them and their families about the possible forms healing might take. I pray for comfort, for the knowledge of the presence of God, and for meaning and wisdom for all patients. I pray for healing for those who understand that their ultimate healing means leaving this world.
—Anne, 39, hospital chaplain and pastor

The Scriptures do not give examples of people who do not age or who are spared the problems of age. As reluctant as the faith community may be to see illness and aging as a gift, it can be one. The aging process slows activity and gives time for thinking and praying. The aging process is a constant reminder that everyone is mortal and must be ready to face death. There are riches of spirit to be unwrapped by accepting the gifts of time and understanding that come with new lifestyles. The larger faith community has a responsibility to help the gifts be unwrapped.

FAITH AND SOCIAL ISOLATION

One of the faith questions facing older adults and their families is how to maintain faith and use their Christian community for support during the aging process. The social isolation that can result from loss of hearing, vision, and mobility presents a challenge to the faith community—both on the local church level and on national denominational levels. The collective understanding, wisdom, and spirituality of older adults is an important resource that the faith community cannot afford to lose. However, it is difficult to come to church when one can't hear or see or sit in hard pews for long periods of time.

Creative Christian faith finds ways to include, not exclude, as aging diminishes the ability of people to participate in the ways they usually have.

I told my parish council that we needed a wheelchair ramp. They said we didn't because we didn't have people in wheelchairs. Well, we don't have people in wheelchairs—or with canes or walkers—because they can't get in the church. [The church] has to be accessible for people to come.

—Glenn, 47, newly called pastor

The decision to invite and encourage continued participation of older persons means making the mechanical and environmental changes that allow them to come, hear, and sit comfortably. Something as simple as a stack of chair cushions can help those who need extra padding for comfort. A good sound system with well-distributed speakers can help those who can't hear, as well as a well-written bulletin that includes the announcements and prayer concerns that will be read aloud. Some of these items are more expensive than others, but almost all are within the reach of churches, especially with the help given by some denominations.

Aside from these physical additions, there is a more important, fundamental need for older adults to know they are wanted and that their desire to continue to worship is honored. The Scriptures are full of examples of older adults being key to the work of God and the gospel.

Anna and Simeon are familiar persons in the story of the baby Jesus. Both were old, both were waiting for the Messiah. They were promised the opportunity to see the Messiah, and both declared that the baby Jesus was this Savior. They already knew what it would take the disciples and others a long time to understand.

God did not use Abraham and Sarah to bring forth the people who would be called Hebrews until they were quite elderly. God continued to have power, presence, and revelation for Abraham and Sarah long after the majority of this culture would have pushed them aside as old and useless.

The Christian community is called to see older adults as persons of differing talents, abilities, gifts, and faith and to make room for and welcome them, whatever the limitations age may be placing on them.

COPING SKILLS

Most older parents are able to cope with their physical problems and often provide younger family members with examples of patience and persistence in the face of difficulty. Kahana and Bibring (1964), in writing to counselors of older adults, identified several types of mechanisms commonly used in coping with physical illness (quoted in Blazer 1990, 186-88). Children of older parents can also use their insights especially in relation to four of these coping mechanisms.

Dependent and overdemanding. One coping mechanism is to become dependent and overdemanding. In this instance the parents want the adult children to take constant care of them and often to tell them what to do and make decisions for them. No matter how much a child does for an older parent, it does not seem to be enough. Adult children can be made to feel guilty for not doing enough and may become angry with their older parents for being unappreciative. Older parents who use this coping mechanism are often unable to face the decisions that must be made concerning their care. New and different illnesses require constant choices, and some older parents are not able to make them.

I used to drive my daughter crazy. I wanted her to come by more and more often, and finally she had to just say to me, "Mother, I'm there three times a week. What more do you want? What do you expect of me?" I was a little embarrassed. I expected her to make it all right again, and she can't. I want her to make it so I can walk, and she can't. She can't replace my legs.

—Elizabeth

Elizabeth's daughter had a good idea, even if borne of frustration and anger. A clear communication about when and how long visits will be, who will take parents where, and what will be the level of decision making can help keep resentments from building up on both sides. Often both older parents and adult children want the impossible, for time to go backwards and have the parents well again. Adjusting to the reality of aging is difficult for both sets of people.

Controlled and orderly. Another mechanism is to become orderly and controlled. Older parents using this coping mechanism might become perfectionists about medicines and medical care and resist any sudden changes or inconveniences. Adult children will find parents needing to control every aspect of their care. Canceled or changed appointments, for example, can be a major crisis. These parents may have unrealistic expectations about their children's abilities to control their medical care. They may become angry or agitated when their doctor must cancel an appointment for an emergency or when an adult child cannot come when promised. This coping mechanism is a response to feeling out of control, sometimes for the first time in their lives. No one can teach someone else how to relax when his or her life is out of control. One possibility is to have discussed in advance alternative plans.

Whenever we take Dad for a doctor's visit, we ask where else he would like to go. We say, "If the doctor has an emergency and has to reschedule, would you like to shop for shoes or to have lunch with Aunt Renee?" We have to plan for every contingency. In his heart Dad would want the doctor to take care of the emergency, but every change upsets him so. We want to plan, plan, plan. He feels like he is in control.

—Wally, 45, son of William

Dramatic and denying. Older parents might also become overly dramatic and need constant approval or attention. In this coping mechanism older parents deny their illness and become anxious when confronted with the reality of their physical problems. Adult children confront their parents' anxiety and perhaps anger when trying to talk honestly with them about the illnesses. One problem is that older parents who are not willing to admit the extent of their medical problems often are not diligent about taking medication, keeping doctor's appointments, or following the doctor's advice. These older parents may choose vanity over assistance, specifically not wanting to be seen with a walker or cane. Overly dramatic patients may emphasize personal appearance more than ever before, or they may want their children to be constantly surprising them with gifts or little favors. These older parents are coping by not dealing directly with the problems. They either shift the focus or deny the existence all together. These older parents may deny the natural deterioration of their body and the assistance they will need in the future. They want to stay in the moment and can no longer project or anticipate. They may also be overly fatalistic.

Self-sacrificing. These older persons regard their illness as one more time in their life when things have gone badly for them. They see themselves as put upon and unfortunately do not always care for themselves well. Adult children of parents in this group will have difficulty getting their parents to the doctor, will often discover that their parents are not following instructions, and may discover that preventable conditions develop from their parents' self-neglect.

I've suffered all of my life. Why should it be different now? I mean I've always had to work hard, and I've given my children everything. Now that I need something, I feel they've deserted me. They act like I'm the crazy one. So what's new? If all else fails, blame Mama.

—Henrietta, 74, retired homemaker

Henrietta is telling the truth about working hard all of her life and giving most of the results of her labor to her children. At the time she did it, though, it was her choice. Her choice continues to be to not pay attention to herself and her needs. Adult children must try to be sure that prescriptions are being filled and taken, knowing such intervention will not be welcomed or appreciated because it threatens the self-suffering stance. This group is most likely to be carrying out a lifelong pattern.

ONE DAY AT A TIME

By far the largest group of older parents are those who have decided to face their illnesses and problems as they come up.

I know a lot of my friends are complaining constantly about their aches and pains. I have my fair share, and sometimes I would give anything to run through the fields again. I can barely walk. My heart, though, runs through those wheat fields with more joy than I ever had as a child because I know what the wheat fields mean. They mean bread for me and for millions of other people. They mean hope that the future will keep on getting better. Give me a young heart and an old body instead of a young body and old heart any day.

—Rebecca

These older parents are well adjusted, and although they may exhibit some of the coping mechanisms discussed above at times, they are willing to continue to take responsibility for their lives and their care.

Good health can continue well after retirement and can be helped by some healthy habits.

1. *Regular sleep schedule.* Insomnia and night waking can be helped by regular sleep schedules. Older adults will have less sleep interruption if they follow a specific routine that includes eating early enough in the evening to have digestion finished by bedtime, going to bed at the same time each evening, and getting up at the same time every morning. Often in preretirement life, older adults had a regular schedule established by their work. Reestablishing a regular schedule will help establish regular sleep.

2. *Daily exercise.* Both the body and the mind need exercise. As bodies slow down, the temptation is to do nothing. Walking is the most highly recommended exercise, and many communities provide walking tracks for older adults. There are also several exercise videos of low-impact aerobic workouts for older adults.

3. *Cut back or eliminate tobacco, alcohol, and caffeine.* Although younger bodies seem to tolerate higher quantities of these addictive substances, they are not healthy at any age. Older parents might find changing long-time habits difficult, but decreased use of these substances can increase energy and aid sleeping.

4. *Create a good environment.* Make an effort to create environments that are conducive to health. Have warm living rooms and moderately cool bedrooms. Be sure that there is fresh air flowing through the ventilation system and good reading lights. Older adults should become selfish when it comes to getting their environmental needs met.

5. *Eat well and drink sufficient quantities of water.* At any age the human body is wondrously made and able to recover

from many illnesses and diseases when given the right help. A family physician can recommend the kind of diet best needed for each person, but all people can benefit from less fat, less sugar content, more fresh fruit and vegetables, and water.

INTERMEDIATE CARE DECISIONS

Most older adults can make fairly good care decisions when presented with the options in a way that is understandable. The decisions may be more emotionally based—on the wants and desires of the older parent—than rationally based. Families struggle when older parents cannot have what they want. Some intermediate care options are:

1. Household help. Household help is one care option that often arises as strength and mobility are affected. The adjustments to this can be difficult for more than the obvious reasons—older parents hate to admit they can no longer do the work they once did and they hate to give up control. Their ability to work is tied to their identity as a man or woman. Also, it is sometimes frightening to have strangers come into the house and do such things as cleaning and laundry. Older parents may feel uncomfortable, especially in larger towns and urban areas where the household worker is almost certainly unknown to them. They may fear theft or personal injury as older adults are often the targets of unscrupulous people. The stories of these events are told again and again by older parents. They may be embarrassed by a lack of control of bodily function that someone else doing the laundry will surely discover.

If possible, an adult child should be in the house with the older person the first few times a new household worker comes. Before the worker comes, adult children can list all the valuables in the house with descriptions and serial numbers or other identifying information. A small home safe to lock up jewelry and other articles is important. Or the valuables can be taken out of the house or apartment. This may also protect household workers from false accusations of stealing items that have been lost or mislaid for many years. Making sure there is a list of all expected duties, the approximate time work is expected to take, and the wages to be paid will help keep communications clear. Some workers have prescribed duties that they can and cannot do, especially if they are being paid by a third party insurance carrier or Medicare. Older parents cannot always remember what wages were promised or, if the pay is through Medicaid or Medicare, what records must be kept. It would be helpful for adult children to assist with or assume this responsibility.

Adult children may want to stop in occasionally for a subtle inspection just as the household worker is supposed to be finishing. Most household helpers are completely honest and hardworking. The biggest possibility for problems with household help is not dishonesty or mistreatment, but that all the work will not be done or done effectively. Again, most household helpers are completely trustworthy, but a small number may become complacent or careless.

2. *Limiting space.* As simple as it seems, one of the best helps for older parents in the face of deteriorating health is limiting the space they are responsible for cleaning. Many older parents automatically start shutting the doors to the spare rooms or only using the downstairs. Adult children might need to suggest this in some instances.

Furniture may need to be rearranged so that older parents can sleep downstairs or don't need to go downstairs to a basement laundry. Even if the rearrangement takes some financial investment, the energy it saves older parents may make their ability to be independent more prolonged.

Adult children might want to approach these changes as helpful to them. For example, telling older parents that they are worried about them falling or that they want them to not take chances on the basement steps. Older parents may be more willing to make concessions based on what will give their children peace of mind rather than admit to limitations they have.

3. *Skilled nursing care.* For limited nursing needs a visiting nurse can often offer the skilled nursing care needed without hospitalization or nursing care facilities. For example, many older parents who have smoked or worked around hazardous chemicals may have breathing difficulties. If they use oxygen, a skilled nurse can monitor their breathing, be sure all the equipment is sterile and working, and do special tasks, such as suctioning or administering medication.

Another example is the changing or monitoring of medication. Sometimes it is easier on family relations to have a skilled nurse do this. Older parents may feel as if their adult children are treating them like children when they ask regularly about medicines.

Adult children may have trouble determining when their parents are having a real life-threatening medical crisis or are panicking. Most adult children develop an intuition about their parents, crises calls. Often the more attentive adult children are to the small crises, the fewer small crises there are.

FINAL CARE DECISIONS

Adult children may have more trouble dealing with the illnesses of their older parents than the older parents themselves. Older parents have experienced firsthand the deterioration of their bodies and have seen family members and friends their age die one at a time. On the other hand, their children may be irritated by all the difficulties of the parents' illnesses and at the same time completely unable to deal with approaching death. It is almost inevitable that any child, of any age, when confronted with the possible loss of a parent begins to feel abandoned.

I confess that I have no idea what I will do when my mother dies. She is so important to me even though we live so far apart. I know she will listen and care and always be there. I have friends and family of my own, but it isn't the same. I hate to think of her being sick and dying. Yet I know she will. Right now her illness is harder on me than it is on her.

—Peggy, 51, daughter of Elizabeth

Older parents and their adult children face grief and the anticipation of death when illnesses begin. Perhaps the best time to discuss eventual care is when death is not imminent.

Medicine is able to prolong heart and lung activity much longer than in previous years, and many older parents have begun already to think about the issues surrounding how they die.

It's important for me to maintain my dignity and not use up all the financial resources of my family. I don't want to lie in a bed unable to live a normal life. No, I don't want that at all. I don't fear dying. I fear what might happen to me before I die.

—Hilda

There are several legal instruments older parents can have that will help direct their medical care if they are unable to do so. Nothing is as important as a family that clearly understands their wishes and is willing to help carry them out. Some important questions for older parents and their adult children to consider are:

1. What level of medical intervention do I want? Many older parents want to receive all possible medical care that will lead to their return to health or to their ability to continue to live lives with a measure of quality. For many the measure of quality has to do with ability to interact with family and friends. Others find quality of life compromised by loss of ability to care for oneself in daily hygiene and eating tasks. When quality of life, as defined by the individual, is no longer possible, there are at least two choices. Does the individual want any possible medical intervention to be made no matter what the quality of life? Does the person want medical intervention in order to be comfortable and free from pain but to allow the natural progress of the final illness toward death?

2. Do I want to be resuscitated if my heart stops? Am I willing to be kept alive by a respirator? Many older adults are willing to have a respirator used for an interval of healing, such as

in intensive care following surgery or illness. Yet these same older adults would not want to be kept indefinitely on a respirator. The same kind of distinction can be made for resuscitation. If the chance of regaining some measure of regular life or some quality of life exists, then it is often seen as an option. When there is no reasonable hope of regaining their quality of life, many patients decide not to prolong death with resuscitation.

3. Do I want artificial nutrition if I am unable to eat? Many people consider the termination of nutrition, whether through a gastric tube or intravenous solutions, the taking of human life. Others consider it ending one more form of medical intervention. States have different laws concerning artificial nutrition. Some do not allow it to be discontinued once begun; others do.

These difficult questions are not easily decided unless family members know what one another wants. The answers might change.

I always said that I didn't want a lot of stuff done to me so that I would just die peacefully without the tubes and wires. Then I had my heart attack. Well, let me tell you, now I want these doctors to do everything they can. Shock me with those paddles as many times as you need. Keep me alive as long as you can. I want every breath I can get.

—Angie, 78, retired teacher and heart patient

Sometimes doctors, ministers, rabbis, or family friends can help facilitate the discussions between older parents and their adult children. There are often religious and community value questions to be included. Older parents will find as they approach a final illness that it is critical that their family and their doctor share their goals and views. Sometimes this requires legal help, discussed in the next chapter.

A Word for the Faithful. Illness and aging create new abilities and new challenges for individuals. There are also gifts and challenges for the faith community. The gifts are the wisdom, talents, and deeper spiritual understanding that come with age. The challenges are to fight social isolation and discouragement. God uses everyone, without regard to age, in God's service. While talking about sickness and aging, the faith community must also be included.

A Prayer for Older Parents. Dear Lord, my ability to do what I want, to hear, to see, and to move about is changing. I don't like the changes, but I understand that no one is exempt from aging. Give me grace and understanding and help me to find ways to continue to learn and grow. Amen.

A Prayer for Adult Children of Older Parents. Dear Lord, help me to find ways to include my parents. Help me to listen carefully, to hear their needs, and to be sure that in their illness and aging they do not feel useless. Lead me to be sensitive to their gifts and receive their wisdom. Amen.

CHAPTER 4

FINANCIAL AND LEGAL PLANNING

The bank called again and I am overdrawn. I added and added and subtracted and subtracted and I can't find my mistake. The bank manager just mentioned that I might consider letting someone help with my finances. They have a service for seniors. When I hung up the phone, I started to shake and then to cry. I hate it when I cry. I don't have much money. I don't want my children to know how little there really is and I certainly don't want a stranger to know. I worked all my life to leave my children something and I have almost nothing left. I feel like a failure. I learned to add when I was a child and now I must ask my child to add for me. Worst of all though is that I don't think I'll be able to afford the care my wife is going to need as we get older. I failed her. I promised I'd always care for her and I've failed her.

—Grady, 82, retired builder

Grady is, unfortunately, not alone in his frustration. He is not incompetent by any means, nor has he failed his wife. He does need help in day-to-day financial matters, such as keeping a bankbook, and may need help in planning for the future if his resources are short. Most older parents are completely able to care for their financial and business matters.

Some need help with items connected to memory, such as remembering to pay bills and remembering to write down checks. However, because older parents have usually spent many years making their own financial decisions, even the best parent-child relationship is strained when children try to take over the financial concerns of their parents.

Sometimes an older parent's spending looks foolish to everyone but the parent. Mentally competent older parents have the right to spend their money foolishly if they so choose, but adult children who constantly question expenditures may make the parent feel defensive. Financial abuse complaints are more common than other forms of elder abuse complaints. This is probably because communication around finances is perhaps more difficult for older parents and their adult children than any other issue. In this culture many individuals have been taught from early childhood to save money, pay their bills, take care of their own finances, and not to trust other people with their money. When one learns to write a check, one is told not to hand those blank checks over to anyone, even a friend, and to be careful with money. The resistance to handing over control to someone else can be overwhelming.

My children seem to think that gray hair means I've lost all ability to think. I got a checkbook with carbons so I don't forget what checks I've given. I have a volunteer with the senior action council that helps me with taxes and things. I don't want to be treated like an idiot, especially by my children. I want them to always think of me as smart. I want to be their mother, not their burden.
—Jeanetta, 89, retired shopkeeper

Adult children often worry about their parents' money because they want to be sure their parents are cared for and have what they need. Other adult children have seen the problems faced by middle-income families when one parent needs full-time care. Many families face eventual full-time nursing care for one or more older parent, and trying to plan ahead for such care can be an anxiety-ridden process. If adult children push for the information needed for such planning, they may be attacked by their parents for being nosey or unfeeling; if they don't, they may be caught with an unbearable financial burden.

Some older parents place a high value on leaving an inheritance for their children and may be unwilling to spend their money for needed care. They see having a little something to leave their children as a matter of personal success. Adult children who try to talk them out of this position are often met with a high level of determination. These older parents are not saying that they feel their children expect an inheritance. Rather, they are saying it is a matter of their sense of pride and personal accomplishment.

FAITH AND MONEY

Money is perhaps the single biggest challenge to faith in this culture. Many people measure their personal worth and success in terms of the things they have acquired, and persons who are poor are generally thought to be stupid, lazy, or impaired in some way. There is no longer a sense that poverty is noble or that being without things shows discipline. This is a huge cultural shift from the time older adults were young. It is also a huge shift in faith. During the last fifty years, since World War II, there has become a stronger and stronger connection of God's blessing with material wealth. It dates back to the Abraham covenant and in the modern interpretation seems to say that people who are poor, who stay poor, and cannot move up are somehow not doing what they should be doing.

While many people intellectually exempt older adults from the stigma of poverty, the cultural messages are still sent and received loud and clear. Having is being. The faith community is called to be a prophetic voice against such misuse of the Abrahamic covenant. Yes, God blesses believers, but not all of those blessings are monetary. The talented artist may have little money but have the joy of creating. The inner-city child may not have money but may have a large extended family that loves and cares for that child. Instead of buying into the culture that says having is being, the faith community needs to strive toward an ethic of sharing with all and letting each person's character and life journey, not income, speak for him or her.

Perhaps more than any other book of the Bible, the Gospel of Luke addresses itself to issues of poverty and wealth. In Luke 16:19-31, the story of Lazarus, the poor man who sat at the gate of the rich man, Jesus changes Abraham's equation of "wealth equals blessing."

> "The poor man died and was carried away by the angels to be with Abraham. The rich man also died and was buried. In Hades, where he was being tormented, he looked up and saw Abraham far away with Lazarus by his side. He called out, 'Father Abraham, have mercy on me, and send Lazarus to dip the tip of his finger in water and cool my tongue; for I am in agony in these flames.' But Abraham said, 'Child, remember that during your lifetime you received your good things, and Lazarus in like manner evil things; but now he is comforted here and you are in agony.'" (Luke 16:22-25)

As the lesson unfolds, the problem for the rich man was that he did not listen to Moses and the prophets, implying that the teachings of mercy and care for the poor were not heeded. Having money is not the problem; what the rich man did with the money was the problem.

Values related to money within a single family can vary greatly. Some may equate financial success with God's blessing; others may see it as a responsibility to live up to the words of the Scriptures about sharing and caring for others. Some may see it as both. Some people see money as something they have earned and as being separate from their spiritual life altogether.

Respect for differences and talking about values and desires is difficult, but it is also the only way to get through the financial adjustments that retirement and aging bring.

FINANCIAL ADJUSTMENTS

Financial concerns change in retirement, and many retiring persons are amazed and dismayed at how little they receive and at how little what they receive will buy. There are some discounts available, but not nearly enough to offset the lower income. It can be disheartening to work all of one's life and then have to scrimp and save and do without basics to live in retirement. It is especially disheartening if adult children continue to expect the same level of financial solidarity. Mom and Dad may not be able to afford to take the grandchildren out to the movies or have the whole financial responsibility for the annual family holiday feast. All the extended family, including the adult children and their families, must adjust.

Statistics on income for older adults can be interpreted in a variety of ways. Most older adults have a greater net worth than younger adults. This average figure, $60,300, is well above the United States average of $32,700 (Waters and Goodman 1990, 20). Net worth though is not the only indicator to consider. Younger adults anticipate earning money for many more years; older adults have passed the peak of their earning power. Older adults must also face extreme expenses in long-term care.

The median income in 1987 for older adults was $11,854 for men and $6,734 for women. This median income is above the poverty line but certainly does not allow for luxuries. The poverty rate for persons over sixty-five was 12.2 percent compared to 10.8 percent for those ages eighteen to sixty-five. Persons over eighty-five years of age are the poorest in the nation (Waters and Goodman 1990, 21).

Most older parents have less disposable income than when they were working, and the future can be uncertain for them. They do not know from one day to the next when an illness will strike or if it will take all their savings. Yet they love their children and grandchildren and want to continue to give to them.

Older parents may find saying no to children and grandchildren particularly difficult and embarrassing. This culture clings to the idea that a man who cannot or has not provided for his family is a failure. With so many women in the workforce and supporting their families, this perception is beginning to be applied to women, too.

I have enough money to live. I have enough for taxes, utilities, groceries, insurance, car repairs, and the like. I have enough for a few extras. My son seems to think that I have a lot of money. He has asked on several occasions to borrow a few hundred dollars. I don't have it to lend. I have a couple of thousand in savings, and I can't use that for him. The rest is tied up in retirement accounts, and if I take it out, my checks each month get smaller. I don't want him to know we live from check to check.

—Ralph

Likewise, it can be dehumanizing to have adult children always pay the check or try to constantly give older parents gifts of money. The balance between understanding and being patronizing can be a difficult one for adult children. Adult children of older parents can find the financial tightrope a difficult one to walk.

My mother is so stubborn. She can't afford to eat out but she won't let us treat her, so I end up cooking when she comes over. I am tired after work and I don't want to cook. I am trapped. If we go out and treat her to dinner, she feels like we are taking care of her. If we go out and let her pay, I know she is short for the rest of the month. If we don't go out, I'm stuck in the kitchen. Sometimes it's easier to just not invite her over. It's awful to say, but I don't know what to do and I don't have the energy to figure it out.

—Andrea, 42, daughter of Maggie Lee

Andrea admits that she finally resorted to buying take-out food, taking it home, and putting it in her own dishes and pretending she cooked in order to have her mother eat with her without fighting about money. This is a tricky compromise and uncomfortable. For some older parents and adult children it is easier to lie about money than to confront their differences and adjustments.

Money is a sensitive issue in this culture for all age groups. People are private about their finances and often trapped in unrealistic expectations. Credit purchases have meant that many people live their work lives in debt, and equity in the family home is the primary asset of many retirees. For parents who have always had money to take care of their own needs and some of their children's needs, it is humiliating for them to reach a time when they cannot spend as they always have. Older parents may feel especially patronized by adult children who approach them as if they suddenly know nothing about money.

Adult children can think of ways to be sensitive to parents that do not put pressure on them to disclose their finances. For example, encourage grandchildren to ask for birthday and holiday gifts that are in a lower price range. If the older parents are not having financial difficulties and want to add to the list, they can. If they are having difficulties, they have options within their price range without having to ask for less expensive gift ideas. Some adult children believe that because it is family, everyone should be willing to talk about money openly. When a lifetime of work and self-image is at stake, it may not be easy to talk about financial needs, even to family members.

Some older parents who grew up during the depression refuse to spend the money they've saved for a rainy day, even when it is pouring, because of their dreams of leaving something to their children. It might be easier on the children for the parents to spend money to meet their needs than to keep the children struggling to see that their parents' needs are met. The parents may not be willing to spend their money.

My mother has a certain amount saved to leave each child, and she will not touch that money. She needs a new hearing aid. The *one she has doesn't meet her needs, but she won't spend even $300 for a new one. I will eventually spend it, but it will be hard on me with three kids in high school to put my hands on $300 that doesn't need to go into a college fund. Then eventually she will die and we'll all inherit money that we don't really want. It doesn't make any sense, but it is who she is, and I'm learning to live with it.*

—Mary, 49, daughter of Rebecca

Other older parents feel their children are not as concerned about the parents' well-being as about the inheritance the children expect. No one can say how true this is and for how many families, but the feeling on the part of at least some older parents is real. Adult children may feel their parents have become distrustful and paranoid. They may even feel they have the right to know their parents' personal financial business. This feeling is not totally unfounded, because the financial well-being of some older parents becomes the responsibility of their children. The critical factors in the right of adult children to know may hinge around the competence of older parents to handle their financial resources and how well the parents seem to be living.

Some questions that adult children might ask themselves about their parents' well-being include:

1. *Do I see basic needs going unmet, and is there reason to believe these needs are unmet for financial reasons?* Many older parents simply have different values and spending habits from their adult children. It is uncomfortable for everyone when either side tries to control how the other side spends money. The worn old bathrobe and slippers may be perfectly fine for older parents who view them almost as old friends and are reluctant to spend money until absolutely necessary, even if the money is available. To adult children the same bathrobe and slippers may look as if their parents are not being cared for. Bathrobes are the business of the persons wearing them, and if

the only problem is a difference in spending values, then most adult children would ease family tensions by learning to keep quiet and give their parents new bathrobes on their birthdays. However, if prescription drugs, good shoes, or warm clothing are not being purchased when genuinely needed, then perhaps adult children should gently inquire into finances. Some older parents have a fear of spending money they may need at a later date because they are so aware of their limited income and savings. In a minority of older parents this fear becomes almost a phobia and they endanger their health by scrimping on heat or medicines.

My daughter and her husband are deeply in debt. I never had a credit card and I never owed anyone more than I could pay. She thinks I'm silly not to get a refrigerator on time payments. I don't want another bill coming every month. I pay the heat and the lights and my property taxes, and I always worry. What if the car blows a tire? I am saving some every month, and if I am lucky I'll have enough to buy a good used refrigerator before this one quits completely. I don't know where she (her daughter) gets it. I tried to teach her to save.

—Jeanetta

The problem is that these two different ways of using money and credit will always clash. Unless Jeanetta is endangering herself, she has the right to save up for her refrigerator and pay for it as she chooses. Many older adults have learned to use credit well, but some never will. To see each other as different, instead of wrong, is a challenge for parents and children at any age.

2. *Is money being spent foolishly or impulsively or are older parents refusing to spend money in comparison to previous spending habits?* Some people have always enjoyed spending money; others have always been thrifty. Adult children might be concerned with a parent's sudden change of spending habits. Older parents who used to enjoy spending money on meals out or new clothes and now do neither might be having financial

problems. Older parents who are spending foolishly, in comparison to their former habits, or impulsively could be letting people take advantage of them. In former times traveling salesmen and door-to-door solicitors preyed on older persons. Now the television brings these offers and pressures into their living room. It is hard for adult children to intervene. Unfortunately, this is sometimes necessary. Older persons are also targets for con artists and thieves. Unethical sales personnel sometimes try to talk older persons into buying things they will not need or want.

As unbelievable as it sounds, my mother just bought a $600 vacuum cleaner. She can't walk without a walker. How did she think she would vacuum? The old one was fine for the housekeeper and me to use. The salesman told her it would make my life easier. He said, "You don't want your daughter to hurt herself taking care of you." The nerve. I am taking it back to him and I'll not only get the $600, I'll get a piece of his backside if you know what I mean. Mother is crying and upset. I am crying and upset. Why can't they just leave her alone?

—Lena, 45, daughter of Arlene, 71

Arlene has a perfectly normal desire to save her daughter the trouble of using the old vacuum. Older parents who must receive physical help from their children, such as help with housework, continue to try to take care of their children by worrying about whether they are doing too much.

I worry about my daughter. She works at her office job and takes care of her own family and then comes over here twice a week to do grocery shopping and cleaning. She shouldn't have to work like that. I don't want her to hurt herself on my account.

—Arlene, 71, retired homemaker

Arlene cared for her own mother until she died. She would never have let anyone tell her not to take care of her, but accepting such care from her own daughter is uncomfortable. Arlene has some money and wants to pay a housekeeper. Her daughter is worried that the money will not last. She knows that she cannot take her mother into her home and that she cannot afford private care. Neither has told the other how she feels.

Adult children are most helpful when they are honest about their concerns and listen to what their older parents are feeling.

3. *Are there other signs of dementia or decreased abilities to make good decisions?* An older parent in need of a guardian or conservator will not usually exhibit this need in only financial areas. Adult children with such a parent would be able to recognize a series of concerns. Forgetting to take medicines or keep important appointments would be one sign. Inability to focus on a conversation for an extended period of time or remember conversations from one day to the next would be another. If adult children feel their parents are perfectly fine except for spending habits and financial concerns, it could be that there is a difference in spending priorities instead of real dementia on the part of the parents. However, real dementia does exist in a minority of older parents, and it can be both heartbreaking and difficult.

Adult children may be dealing with the effects of memory loss or dementia of some kind in their parents. If this is true, then the older parents may be both unable to handle their finances and unable to make a reasonable decision to hand financial matters over to their children. Adult children feel they are not trusted, but the distrust is not personal. Later life dementia can lead to the distrust of all people. If the dementia is caused by Alzheimer's disease, then the parent may not even know who his or her children are.

I took mother to the bank. I could see that she was slipping day by day. The doctor had diagnosed Alzheimer's disease, and I knew she would need extra care. I explained three times that I wanted her to consider putting one of the CDs in my name as well as hers so that I could have access to the money she might need. I don't have the resources to care for her while I go through

the court process to have her declared incompetent. She signed over three CDs and talked on and on, very lucidly, about my caring for her. Then she called the police and tried to have me arrested for stealing her money. It was humiliating. Finally, we talked to the bank officer who helped us, and everything was okay.
                              —Lottie, 55, daughter of Frances, 81

While this is a dramatic example, the emotions at work are common. Frances is no longer as competent as she once was, but she has many lucid moments. She has the idea that Lottie is wanting to pay her own debts with her mother's money. Lottie does have a burden of debt and Frances's money could make her life significantly better, but she has no intention of getting it under false pretenses. Lottie would be glad to spend every penny of Frances's money, and her own, to care for her mother. How can they have a common meeting ground?

A third, nonfamily member, such as a guardian, conservator, or trustee can be appointed to help watch Frances's money and be sure her needs are met. This need not be an expensive proceeding if both older parent and adult child agree on who can be trusted. Sometimes, though, these processes are expensive, long, and painful to both parent and child.

Joint checking accounts are also a possibility. This means that either the older parent or adult child can write checks. The older person has control over assets and help in making out payments, and the adult child has some knowledge of the financial circumstances of his or her parent. Also, copies of statements can be sent to the adult child (or older parent) when the other is paying the bills.

Secondary party notices and budget plans. Many banks and utility companies offer secondary party notices that will let an adult child know if accounts are overdrawn or utilities are not paid. Forgetfulness is a natural occurrence in later life and the primary cause of most of the smaller financial difficulties. Often fuel companies and other utilities also offer budget plans in which the older adult can pay the same amount each month so planning is easier. Some offer automatic withdrawal from accounts so older adults do not even have to remember to write out checks.

REVERSE MORTGAGES

Some states have enacted laws that allow banks and other lending institutions to offer what is called a reverse mortgage. The bank makes payments to the homeowner in a certain amount each month, up to a certain level that can be secured by the home. When the homeowner dies, the home is sold and the bank is paid back for the money advanced.

Some life insurance policies offer an advance payment to terminally ill persons, which is taken out of the value of the insurance payment when the person's heirs collect the insurance.

Both of these options can help older parents have more income while they are alive and need it.

ENTITLEMENTS

Besides the obvious concerns around budgeting and inflation for older parents on a fixed income, adult children may also be concerned about eventual full-time nursing care and how to get the most help from government entitlements, such as Medicare, Medicaid, and Social Security.

Medicare. Medicare pays a certain fee for each kind of service performed. Such a fee is usually below the actual charge for medicine, and many older adults must either pay the difference from meager retirement income or pay premiums for private insurance to supplement Medicare. Medicare has no prescription drug coverage at this time.

My wife and I make $765 from Social Security each month. My prescription drugs cost $500. If we did not have savings to draw on, we would be deciding between heart medicine and food. I

don't know what we'll do when the savings run out. I hate going to my kids or selling the house. Some of my friends have recommended putting the house in my son's name so I can get Medicaid, too. Medicaid pays for prescriptions and Medicare won't. It feels like I'm tricking the government. Who knows what will happen to me. Work hard all your life and then worry about buying heart medicine or bread. Why try?
—Judd, 73, retired farmer

Judd has hit on a problem many older parents face. What is the best way to spend the resources he has? Judd's wife, Helene, has a small Medicare supplement policy through her former employer. Her prescriptions are paid for by this policy. Judd wonders if he should try to get a policy but believes the premiums would cost as much as the medicine.

Another Medicare concern often raised is whether or not Medicare will pay enough. Sometimes the only doctors who will take Medicare patients are not the doctors that older parents would choose. They may end up going to a doctor they would not choose because he or she will accept whatever Medicare pays as full payment.

Adult children who sense their parents are unhappy with their doctor and yet reluctant to change might ask if the doctor accepts as payment in full whatever Medicare allows. There may be additional help available or other payment options. Many doctors are happy to accept a monthly payment from older patients, but their patients are used to paying for services as they are given and may be uncomfortable or embarrassed to ask for such a plan.

Medicaid. States put different requirements on Medicaid recipients, so it is important that older parents and their adult children know what these requirements are. Often there are Medicare and Medicaid staff members who can explain these without charge. It can be prudent for real property or assets and investments to be placed in the name of someone other than the older parent. Older parents are sometimes reluctant to take such measures. They may feel this is "cutting corners" and perhaps unfair, or that Medicaid is some form of welfare and they do not want to take welfare. In the long run, older parents may feel that the steps needed to qualify for Medicaid are not worth what they would receive in return. However, if full-time nursing care becomes necessary, Medicare, and most family resources, may not be enough. Even if no action is needed immediately, adult children might want to make a point of understanding the exact workings of Medicare and Medicaid.

Older parents cannot avoid penalties if they apply for Medicare within thirty-six months of the last gift of assets they made to their children (or to someone else). This may induce some people to make gifts way in advance of needing nursing home care. Many of the better nursing homes will not take patients unless they have enough assets to pay for six to nine months of care. An alternative to early gifts is waiting until the nursing home care is necessary and then gifting all but what is needed for the first thirty-six months of care (or even a few extra months) to avoid applying for Medicaid within the thirty-six-month period. Medicaid and Medicare requirements and rules change often, so an attorney who is an expert in Elder Law should be contacted before any irreversible planning decisions are made.

Social Security. Most persons who work have paid enough Social Security taxes to receive some benefits. Many widows receive benefits based on their husband's pay into the system. Benefits increase as people postpone receiving them. For example, a sixty-two-year-old retiree will receive less than a sixty-five-year-old or seventy-year-old retiree. The reasoning for this is that payments to a sixty-two-year-old will be made for more years than those to older retirees. Retirees need to consider their long-range needs as well as their immediate ones when planning retirements.

WILLS AND ESTATES

Most older parents long ago made their wills. As they get older there are additional considerations and their plans may change.

Joint property. The traditional arrangement is that property is held in both persons' names and automatically goes to the survivor. Once a spouse dies, the surviving spouse may want to change his or her estate planning to be more specific. If all property is held jointly with rights of survivorship, probating a will may not be necessary according to state laws. Joint property is not advised for those couples with more than $600,000 in assets, because it cuts down on estate-planning opportunities. For most couples, the joint property arrangement is appropriate.

Some older adults choose to give a child joint rights of survivorship on certain pieces of property in order to simplify the arrangements that will have to be made after death. Others have a hard time deciding how to divide their personal tangible property and leave those decisions to an executor. Usually an executor is only asked to decide on who gets such personal property or how to divide the shares of the other estate property.

Life estates are another option for property. Older persons may deed or sell property to another person, usually a child or relative, while retaining a lifelong right to live in the house or use the assets of the life estate.

Retirement benefits. Retirement accounts are regulated by federal law. Only the surviving spouse can inherit unless that spouse signs a waiver. Some retirement plans give employees the opportunity to decide whether or not to provide benefits for surviving spouses. Providing benefits for a surviving spouse will lower the amount of retirement available each month, because some is set aside for the surviving spouse. In making wills it is important that the exact terms of various retirement plans be considered.

Choosing an executor. If the estate does not pass entirely by right of survivorship, then there will be a probate proceeding and an executor will see to the business of the estate until everything is distributed. Many executors choose to serve without a fee, but most states provide for a fee. If the executor is to serve without a fee, that should be made clear from the beginning. Most older parents appoint a child to be the executor. The executor needs to have easy access to the attorney for the estate and be trustworthy.

Specific property bequests. Many older parents wish to make specific bequests to children. Some states encourage these to be made in a letter to the executor. Letters are usually not legally binding and are used when persons making the bequest are certain they can trust the executor to carry out their wishes. Other bequests are put in the will and the executor is instructed to pay the expenses of shipping the items, the insurance on them, and so forth out of the estate as a deductible administration expense. The manner in which specific property bequests are made are largely a matter of the size of the estate, the value of the tangible property, and the possible involvement of estate or gift taxes. The cost of distribution of bequests in a will may lower the net amount of the estate and thus lower the taxes. Other parents may leave property to their children in such a manner as the children agree upon, with the executor settling disagreements.

Older parents know their wishes and sometimes fear arguments among their children around items they will leave in their estate. Some parents give items to specific children in advance of their deaths to be sure that they retain control of who gets what. It seems straightforward to the parents, but sometimes adult children have specific desires or wants they may make known to their parents. If parents wish to insure that certain items will go to specific people, a legal document of some kind must be executed.

Large estates, trusts, generation-skipping, estate taxes, and predeath gifts. The larger the estate, the more careful legal planning needs to be done. If no will exists, each state has different laws about who receives what. Anyone with an estate of more than $50,000 in assets should be sure that an attorney is consulted and a will signed. The larger the estate the more important it is to seek legal counsel. Trusts can be established or pre-death gifts made to lessen taxes. This is very important for estates where combined assets of the couple exceed $600,000. There are also special deductions with respect to taxes on gifts to grandchildren that allow the inheritance to skip a generation without a generation-skipping tax (a tax on gifts to grandchildren that some people used to make to avoid inheritance tax) applying.

Older parents with considerable assets will probably readily recognize the need for complex legal planning. Adult children may wish assets were not tied up in trusts or want older parents to take a particular course of action. Whatever the asset level of older parents, it is important that they are comfortable with their plans and that they have sought the advice needed to make those plans.

Adult children often need to know that their parents have taken care of the estate planning and wills, but it may be hard for them to ask. They may feel like they will appear to be greedy, and indeed some older parents may believe they are, if they ask about details of inheritances and planning. Money and death are perhaps the two most sensitive issues that adult children and their parents approach together, so this kind of planning is both essential and emotional. Another emotional issue revolves around second marriages and prenuptial agreements.

PRENUPTIAL AGREEMENTS

Many older parents entering second marriages do not make prenuptial agreements but rather use their wills to make sure that both their new spouses and their children inherit appropriately. In the event of a death of an older parent, a will is a perfectly acceptable form for making one's wishes known.

However, in the event of a divorce in a second marriage, a

will has no power to limit the assets taken by the second spouse in a divorce settlement. Older parents who are remarrying may choose to enter into a prenuptial agreement. Often these agreements limit the inheritance of the second marriage partner. Because of community property laws in many states, a prenuptial agreement can be useful in limiting the property settlement for a second spouse. Older parents may be tempted to assume their second marriage will be as rewarding and long lasting as their first one, but second marriages do have a greater risk of divorce, statistically, and are often more challenging to make work.

Prenuptial agreements may be particularly useful if one spouse has considerably more assets than the other and those assets were in part earned by the deceased spouse. The deceased spouse's share of such assets might be considered to rightfully go to that person's children rather than to a second spouse. Family trust funds, businesses, or properties often are placed in the category of assets to be protected from divorce settlements by a prenuptial agreement. Older parents might select to deed the property to the children before the second marriage in lieu of a prenuptial agreement.

Most older parents want to be sure their second spouses are comfortable and cared for after they have died. Adult children may not recognize the importance of this goal immediately, but a combination of premarriage gifts, prenuptial agreement, and estate planning can be used to make the wishes of the older parent clear.

The advantage of a prenuptial agreement might be to cut out jealousy or suspicion on the part of adult children. Older parents may use such an agreement to assure their children that the inheritance from their dead parent is secure.

POWERS OF ATTORNEY

A power of attorney is a legal document that gives one or more people, as individuals or as a group, the ability to make decisions for the person granting the power of attorney.

General powers of attorney. A general power of attorney grants broad rights for an indefinite period of time. These are usually short, two-page documents that are easy to transact. These are often used by older parents as they reach an age where incompetence or debilitating illness are possibilities. Often the powers are kept for many years, unused, until the person granting them becomes unable to make decisions for him- or herself. Each state has different laws about the forms of such powers of attorney. Some states require this form of power of attorney for the transfer of real property.

Limited powers of attorney. A power of attorney that does not grant broad powers may be given for specific reasons. There are two ways to limit powers of attorney. One way is to limit how long the power of attorney is in force. For example, if an older parent is undergoing surgery that might make the parent unable to take care of business or personal concerns for some time, the power of attorney given to a son or daughter would limit his or her actions to the time the parent is in the hospital or to the length of time recovering in the hospital and at home combined.

Another way to limit a power of attorney is to limit the kinds of activity that the power can be used to carry out. A power of attorney may allow only business or banking transactions or only transactions relating to a specific asset or piece of property.

Durable powers of attorney. Some states have durable powers of attorney that remain in effect even when the granter becomes disabled. These can be very important so that assets remain within the reach of spouses and adult children who may be in charge of an older parent's care.

LAST ILLNESS DOCUMENTS

While many persons die following quick illnesses or in accidents, others have longer illnesses and have to face questions about medical care. Many older persons choose to limit the kinds of medical care they receive and how long they continue to receive care in the case of their last fatal illness. A final illness may last many years or only a few weeks. This is defined by the medical community's best estimate of what will happen. The medical personnel are saying that in all likelihood the illness now suffered will result in death. When a patient is close to dying, many people in the medical community believe that prolonging the time of the illness is prolonging death instead of life. Other people believe that every minute of life is precious and every measure should be taken to lengthen life, whatever the quality of that life. Most documents relating to final illness are made by people who do not want their illness prolonged. Anyone with strong feelings about the kind and duration of medical care they receive should consider making those wishes known. These are legal documents, signed, notarized, and given to doctors and others who will make care decisions.

Living wills. The most common document is a living will. This gives specific instructions concerning levels of medical care. Most older parents do not fear death so much as they fear the indignities of long-term medical care and the drain it causes on the financial resources of the family. Their values do not put length of life, sometimes artificially maintained, above quality of life.

The medical phrase often used to designate a last illness is "no reasonable hope of recovery." Most living wills borrow this terminology and urge that when there is no reasonable hope of recovery, certain medical treatments or measures not be taken.

No resuscitation following heart failure is a common request of terminally ill patients. This order, which must be expressed by the patient either directly or through a document such as a living will, is put on the charts and commonly abbreviated DNR for "Do Not Resuscitate."

Another common request is no use of respirators. In some states once these breathing machines are put into use they cannot be disconnected. The decision not to use a respirator should be made early in the course of an illness.

Artificial nutrition is another category of care that persons may wish to control. Many states do not allow artificial nutrition, whether intravenous or through a nasal tube, to be discontinued once begun. This decision, more than do not resuscitate or no respirator orders, is more difficult for some people to make. The same is true with artificial hydration. Unless a person specifically requests no artificial nutrition or hydration, these measures are taken as a matter of routine. Some doctors recommend that hydration be allowed in all instances to keep the patient more comfortable.

Most patients instruct their medical personnel that they are to receive enough pain relief to keep them comfortable at all times. Many times this pain relief is in the form of morphine, and higher and higher levels of morphine may be needed to relieve pain. The trade-off with pain relief can be alertness, ability to communicate, and loss of concentration. Some older parents request no pain relief for a certain time so they may speak clearly and directly to their families. Older parents who are conscious and competent need to be allowed to weigh the advantages of heavy drug therapy against the disadvantages and make their own decisions.

Whatever the wishes of the older parent, they should be stated clearly in a document and copies of the document given to each physician. Older parents should also give copies of their living will to the persons most likely to be talking to physicians about the older parent's care. The parents might also make a health-care proxy or medical power of attorney, which gives the adult child the authority to make sure their wishes are carried out, usually where the patient is unconscious or unable to communicate or otherwise make decisions. States have different regulations concerning the types and forms of these documents. Both attorneys and doctors can give advice on such documents. While the struggle with income and financial decisions may increase with age, so do wisdom and experience. The next chapter explores wisdom, mentoring, and spirituality.

A Word for the Faithful. Financial and money problems are difficult. Adult children want their parents taken care of, well fed, with good medical care and comfortable, safe housing. As urban neighborhoods change and costs of living go up, there are many challenges to meeting this goal. Sometimes God is the last place adult children and their older parents look for help. Praying for guidance and help is the first step, not a last resort.

A Prayer for Older Parents. Dear God, for so much of my life you have cared for me and given me work to do to earn the money I need. I can no longer care for my needs through labor and am looking to you to show me the path to take. Give me wisdom with the resources I have and help me to understand the love and blessings that are a part of this stage of my life. Amen.

A Prayer for Adult Children of Older Parents. Dear God, remind me each day of your love and compassion and help me not to be judgmental about my parents' patterns of saving and spending. Help me to know your way and your truth and to deal gently with the disagreements and difficulties that may arise. Amen.

CHAPTER 5

SPIRITUALITY AND MENTORING

I look at my little grandchildren and think of all they have to face in their lives. I think of all I have faced and know I could not have done it without the Lord's strength. I wish I could just open up those little minds and pour into them all the faith and love I know and all the things I've learned. I hope they come to me when they need me.

—Naomi, 71, retired transit worker

Naomi feels the frustration of many parents and grandparents. They know the road ahead for the children in their families is filled with challenges, adventures, heartache, celebrations, boredom, and hard times. One of the strengths of age is the level of experience—experience that is not always understood or appreciated.

The knowledge gained in a life's journey is a precious gift. Sometimes, though, the means of communication doesn't make the knowledge readily usable. Older parents tend to communicate their experiences by telling their life stories to a generation that is used to communicating through the Internet and multimedia. A simple story may not, at first, appear to have importance.

EXPERIENCES OF A LIFE JOURNEY

The challenge for families and faith communities is in how to use the experiences of their older members to learn, to live better lives, and to show one another new possibilities.

The other day my grandson came home from Sunday school with a special prize for learning a Bible verse. He went on at great length about how he didn't know why he had to learn Bible verses since he had a Bible, but he did what the teacher said anyway. Suddenly I realized that I must know a hundred different Bible verses by heart. I began to say the ones I remembered, and my grandson's eyes got so big. I told him how in World War II I had no Bible with me and in the middle of the battles I would repeat those verses I knew over and over. I told him that learning the verses gave me the Bible in my heart. He was so impressed. It felt good to impress him.

—Jonathan, 76, retired teacher

Jonathan's grandson learned more than the importance of Scriptures in that conversation. He also learned about a war that ended long before he was born, and about the importance of faith to his grandfather. He became connected in another way to a different time.

The experiences of older parents are the gardens in which the future has been planted and cultivated. The experiences of World War II began, among other things, to change the way women were viewed in the workforce. The Vietnam War appeared on televisions everywhere, and the culture began to see a side of war previously known only to soldiers.

Just as national experiences shaped the nation's future, individual experiences shaped persons and families. The depression shaped many families' ethics and habits around saving, spending, and sharing money because it left such a mark on the lives of older parents.

I was a young mother when the depression came. I couldn't do much for my family, so I felt like a failure. Then during the war I traded gasoline rationing coupons for sugar and other coupons. We lived in the city and didn't need them. I remember the pride I felt that my children had sugar. When I see my daughter throwing out food because she cooked too much or cooking something different for my granddaughter because she doesn't like the family meal, I wonder if they know how lucky they are not to be worried about having enough to eat. I want to say to them, "Look how lucky you are. You don't worry about food. Thank God for that." But I know they would just think I was a silly old woman living in the past.

—Naomi

That is the challenge for older parents and for the people who love them. How can these experiences be transformed into knowledge that aids and educates? If knowledge gained in the past enriches the present and the future, then women like Naomi are not living in the past but using it.

KNOWLEDGE THAT TEACHES

One of the ways that experience and knowledge teach is by opening up cross-generational understanding. Many families have habits, events, or customs that occur or are passed on through succeeding generations. For example, alcoholism is usually a multigenerational problem. Other patterns of relationships, such as an overattachment between fathers and youngest daughters or mothers and oldest sons, may also cross many generational lines.

My grandmother married her cousin's husband after her cousin died tragically. My great-great-grandmother married her sister's husband after her sister died. I married my aunt's first husband. I didn't know that there was this odd kind of habit in our family until I was talking to Gram one day. I don't know yet what it means—except that we have always had a close extended family and we all know one another. What other families might have considered weird, like marrying a relative's husband, was acceptable to us. I wonder if there are other little tidbits of information I'm missing. Gram also told me that the hardest time for her was when her first child was born and she felt guilty because both she and the baby were fine while her cousin had died in childbirth. My aunt was killed in a car accident. I have sometimes felt guilty for being alive.

—Sara-Jean, 26, graphic artist

Sara-Jean discovered an interesting multigenerational habit in her family. Some such habits are heartbreaking, some are informative, some are healing. Adult children can help their parents' knowledge be a teaching knowledge in several ways.

1. *Ask questions about stories.* The temptation when you hear a story for the third (or thirty-third) time is just to wait until it is over. Telling the same story again and again could have two meanings. One is that older parents may not remember having told it. Or, more importantly, it may mean that the story is an invitation to learn more, but the older parents just can't quite bring themselves to say more without encouragement. Stories told again and again often deal with an unresolved issue or struggle. Some leading questions are:

Is there something about this that still troubles you?

Would you do/say anything differently now?

What would you want me to do in the same situation?

How do you feel about it now?

When my sister was murdered, I couldn't eat or sleep or speak for days. I just couldn't imagine how that could happen to her, to my family. They found her body near the railroad and everyone said that some transient did it. That was in 1933, and nobody thought about someone in town being that kind of person, I mean a killer and all.

—Dick, 86, retired judge

When Dick's daughter and pastor heard the story of the murder for the tenth time, they asked Dick an important question: What do you think happened? Dick's response startled them and himself.

I have never told another living soul this. I think her boyfriend killed her. I think she wanted to get married and he didn't and they had a fight. I think he went right on living in our town, smiling at me and my family and coming to her funeral. [Dick begins to weep.] I think he hit her on the head with a rock in a spurt of temper and then just left her. They used to walk by that railroad track. I used to see them from the window of my room.

—Dick

In hearing these words, Dick's daughter realized that the many times she had found him critical of her dates and all of the times they had argued that some young man was not good enough for her, a dark fear had been in her father's heart. This explained so much to her.

I confess. I used to almost hate him. Of course, I'm sixty-two years old now and that's all water under the bridge, but I can remember how angry I was. I let my own daughter date several men I didn't like just because I was determined not to be like my father.

—Joyce, 62, attorney

The power of a secret—whether the story of an event or a feeling—can often influence a person's actions in ways that other people can't understand. Sharing knowledge becomes a teaching experience when secrets are revealed.

2. *Look for new previously undisclosed details.* Many times when a story is told over and over new details are added. Most police interrogators know this and have witnesses go over their stories again and again until they are sure everything has been remembered. A new detail or fact can be a valuable clue as to why the story is so important to the older parent.

My son looked for weeks to find a good used car for me that I could afford. I wrecked the other one. Then when I had had it less than a year, it got to where it wouldn't start. Then one day it just quit running. I had to walk five blocks to the garage and ask them to come back and get it and fix it, and it took all my extra money.

—Rebecca, retired farmer

Rebecca's son heard the story so many times that he was getting angry. He took the story to be a criticism of the car he had chosen. He wanted to tell her it would be a "cold day in hell" before he helped her pick out another car, but he kept quiet. One day she added some information. She told him she was proud that she remembered where the garage was and that she could walk that far. "I even knew to tell [the mechanic] which warning light was on in the car," Rebecca said proudly. This was a new fact.

It turned out that my mother was trying to show me that she was independent and could walk to the garage and take care of the repairs. She was proud that she had been able to handle the emergency. I forget how much Dad did for her and how helpless she sometimes feels since his death. We think of our parents as a unit and forget that as individuals they contributed different gifts and abilities to the marriage. I asked her if there were other things she would like to be able to do for herself. What a door that opened!

—Harold, 46, grocery store manager

Often older parents are not able to speak directly to children about concerns, fears, and needs. They have been the strong, able ones for so long that to depend on their children is difficult for them. Rebecca learned that she was stronger than she thought. At the same time, Harold learned that he needed to be sure his mother was able to do all she needed to do.

3. *What would you change if you could change the story?* Many older parents have unspoken regrets, especially around

issues of parenting. Sometimes the stories told over and over about an incident in childhood are a way of looking for forgiveness.

Parents are aware now through television and magazines that "parenting" can be done in right and wrong ways. Many parents from two generations back just did what their parents had done. Now they may believe they were wrong.

My mother keeps asking me if she ever did something that I felt was wrong or that I hated her for. At first I really didn't understand why she was asking this question, then I realized that she probably felt she had. When I asked her if she remembered anything she wished she hadn't done, she immediately told me a story of making me go to school when I had a little fever because she was just too tired to deal with a sick child that day. I don't even remember it. It must not have hurt me, but it certainly stayed on her mind all these years. She wanted forgiveness.

—Barbara, 61, veterinarian

Whether it's a desire to tell a family secret, to be understood, or to be forgiven, there are often hidden messages in the stories passed on by older parents.

FAITH AND KNOWLEDGE

First Corinthians 13 has two clear messages for the faith community concerning knowledge. First, it says that knowledge without love is useless, of no value. Second, it says that knowledge is incomplete.

> For we know only in part, and we prophesy only in part; but when the complete comes, the partial will come to an end. When I was a child, I spoke like a child, I thought like a child, I reasoned like a child; when I became an adult, I put an end to childish ways. . . . Now I know only in part; then I will know fully, even as I have been fully known. (1 Corinthians 13:9-12)

Knowledge is limited by the motives of those who use it. It

is also age related. What cannot be understood at six years of age may be understood at sixteen, or it may not be understood until the age of seventy-six. Each age has a different ability to accept knowledge, to hear, and to learn.

There is a challenge in respecting and honoring older adults while at the same time understanding that they are human and may have pasts and attitudes that aren't the ideal of a distinguished elderly person. The need for forgiveness may be even more acute as death approaches and older parents feel there is unfinished business to be resolved.

Forgiveness is not only a blessing for the one who has sinned, but it frees the person who is doing the forgiving from an immense amount of rage and depression. Neither of these outcomes is the reason for forgiveness. Christians are commanded to forgive as a part of their relationship to God. To not forgive is to endanger both that relationship and further spiritual growth.

> "Pray then in this way:
> Our Father in heaven,
>   hallowed be your name.
> Your kingdom come.
> Your will be done, on earth as it is in heaven.
> Give us this day our daily bread.
> And forgive us our debts,
>   as we also have forgiven our debtors.
> And do not bring us to the time of trial,
>   but rescue us from the evil one.
> For if you forgive others their trespasses, your
> heavenly Father will also forgive you; but if you
> do not forgive others, neither will your Father
> forgive your trespasses." (Matthew 6:9-15)

The truth of this passage is not always pleasant and certainly not easy. The message is clear, though; if a Christian is to be forgiven, that Christian must be a forgiver. In family life this is particularly important. How much more of anyone's story could be told if there was no fear—of being laughed at, misunderstood, or unforgiven?

The challenge of First Corinthians is to put knowledge in its place, as incomplete and subordinate to love. The challenge of the Matthew passage is to forgive for the sake of one's own relationship to God without regard to remorse or repentance.

MENTORING FOR THE FUTURE

A television commercial that ran in early 1997 told older parents that they deserved a good retirement because they had done so many things. One of the lines says, "Because you've built more in your life than in the five thousand years before you." No century in recent times has seen so many changes. The commercial focused on cities and buildings. However, the real test of how well a generation has built for the future is in the character and values they have taught their children. Mentoring takes many forms.

Mentoring as teaching. When mentoring is mentioned, immediately most people think of teaching skills or ideas. That is certainly one form of mentoring, but it may not be the most useful form for many people. Teaching is a gift, and just because someone has gotten older doesn't mean that person has become a teacher. Teaching requires patience, an understanding of the learning process, and good communication skills. An older adult who is a teacher will continue teaching.

Teaching can be done in a formal or organized setting. Many churches offer small group experiences, and many communities offer learning programs through community centers. Both give older adults the opportunity to teach others. In these settings most teaching is done informally, where people get together on a one-to-one basis.

I learned to whittle when I was a child. I can use a knife and piece of wood to make almost anything. My son learned, too, but he's afraid to let his boy use a knife without an adult present, and he just doesn't have a lot of time. So, I'm showing him.

Every time he comes over I have a different little project for him to do and we talk about school and his little girlfriend and all sorts of things.

—Gene, 69, retired railroad worker

Other older adults may find in a different kind of mentoring an important contribution they can make.

Mentoring by example. Although methods of doing things change as years pass, an older adult may be able to help a younger one through the maze of personal and professional life by being an example.

I am single and I have no role models of single women in my family. All my aunts and sisters are married. I am also in social work, which is a different area of work than my other family members. But in my church I found a single woman, sixty-four years old, who had spent her life in inner-city social work, just as I plan to do. She helped me through so many rough patches professionally—giving me support in my struggle to leave my job at the office and helping me to adjust to being alone in a world of couples and families. She knew what I was facing professionally and personally. She believed in me and gave me her wisdom.

—Janet, 39, social worker

Janet's mentor would not have claimed so much credit.

I don't know that I did so much. I just knew, though, that it is easy for single people to get so involved in their work that it becomes their whole lives, and I wanted to see Janet with a more well-rounded life. I wanted her to have the same kind of friends and activities that I have had. I also wanted her to see that you don't have to take on all the problems you see on the job. I am a happy person with no regrets. I know I have missed a lot by not having a husband and children, but it just didn't happen, so instead of being sad, I learned to celebrate what I did have. This is what I wanted for Janet.

—Beverly, 71, retired social worker

The key to mentoring by example is that mentors have to be pleased with their lives and aware of the decisions they made to bring them to that point. This kind of mentoring requires honesty and openness about one's life and an ability to see both the good and bad parts.

Mentoring through prayer. A third kind of mentoring isn't thought about much. It is not a direct relationship to others in the same way that mentoring by teaching or example is, although there may be a very close direct relationship. Mentoring by prayer is a way for older adults to use their faith.

I had had a perfectly awful week at the hospital. I had to take an extra floor because one of the chaplains was sick, and I had three very difficult deaths to deal with on my own floors. I saw by my computer printout that there was a woman in for surgery who was from my denomination, and I really wanted to see her. Three or four days passed and I still had not made it in. Finally, I got into the room and she greeted me with "At last you are here." I felt so bad and began to apologize for taking so long when she stopped me. "No," she said, "I mean I have been asking God for a young minister to pray for, and here you are." It seemed that she was a retired missionary and she felt her retirement calling was to pray for young ministers, especially young women, to help them do what they were called to do. She prayed for me right then and promised to continue praying for me. We are not in touch—she said when she left the hospital that her mission was to pray for me, not burden me with a friendship. I know when I am having a bad day that she is praying for me. I know when I'm having a good day that she is praying for me. I wish I had had the friendship. I'm sure it would have been no burden.

—Cynthia, 43, American Baptist minister

Cynthia's mentor has given her a great gift—the knowledge that she has constant spiritual support. While this is less personal in that Cynthia and her mentor do not have daily contact, the mentor knows exactly what it is like to be a servant of God, and may know more about Cynthia's deepest needs than Cynthia even knows.

Another way to mentor through prayer is by close contact.

My parents pray for me each day. They pray for me and for each of my brothers and sisters. I used to joke that I had to behave myself every night at 10 P.M. because I knew that was when they had their daily devotions and prayers. My mom has always been the first phone call I make when I need help. I know that she is older, and Dad has died already. I don't know what I'll do when she goes. I guess I'll find some other dear heart who has enough love of God to pray for me.

—Linda, 39, restaurant manager

Linda's prayer mentor knows her needs and desires. This is a more personal form of prayer mentoring and one many older adults prefer because they also treasure the closeness and companionship. Prayer mentoring is possible in another way.

I was on my way to dinner with friends when I passed a young man on crutches who was begging for food outside a grocery store. I usually gave food when asked, but I was in a hurry, so I rushed past him. All through the dinner I thought of this young man and knew it was God's will that I help him, yet I had passed him by. After dinner I walked back to the store, and he was still there. We went inside, and I bought him about $10 worth of eggs and milk and bread—less than I had just spent on one meal for myself. As we walked out of the store, he asked me my name. He pulled out his New Testament and wrote my name in it. He promised to pray for me every day. Since then I've realized that his commitment to me brings me to have a commitment to him. I know what a young parent faces and how hard employment can be. I am praying for his life even as he prays for mine.

—Julia, 76, retired nurse

Mentoring by prayer can be a gracious thanksgiving for all the blessings of a lifetime and can grow out of a deep spiritual commitment to help those who are younger in the faith. Julia has a face and a story to go with the person she prays for, but that isn't necessary. Every young man and woman, every middle-aged man and woman, every child needs prayer. Some Christians have decided to pray according to the day or season for people they do not know by name but who they know are experiencing the problems of being a Christian. For example, one older woman prays for all religious workers and ministers on Sundays, for all school teachers on Mondays, for all business and professional workers on Tuesdays, for all parents on Wednesdays, for all medical workers on Thursdays, for all government workers and leaders on Fridays, and for all retired and disabled persons on Saturdays. She is specific and compassionate in her prayers. This kind of mentoring grows out of a spirituality that is based on years of Christian journey.

SPIRITUALITY THAT STRENGTHENS

Another product of growing older is often growing more spiritual in the way one looks at the world. Every older Christian has not only had a tremendous number of experiences in the world but also a tremendous number of experiences with Christ.

The condition of the soul. All Christians have stories of how they came to believe, to be forgiven, and to accept God's presence and power in their lives. How can adult children talk about the condition of their parents' souls?

Before he died, my daughter asked her father how he felt about God these days as his life had changed so much in the past few years. He said clearly that he was angry at God because of his illness, but that he was sure God was real and that God understood his anger. I never knew he felt that way. I was able to say that I was feeling separated from God and that prayer was hard for me. The three of us talked for over an hour about our feelings for God. We all felt closer to God.

—Ellie

While it was Ellie's daughter who was worried about God in her parents' lives, often the roles are reversed and older parents are questioning their children about spiritual matters.

My son, however, is a different matter. I don't know when God will answer my prayers, but I just keep praying that he will come back to God and the church. I don't talk to him about it anymore, though, because I don't want him to be angry. I just pray every day for God to mean as much to him as he does to me.

—Ellie

Some questions older parents and children might share about conditions of the soul are common for all times and ages.

1. Are you growing in your relationship to God? Are you closer to God now than before? Christians never stop changing and growing spiritually. The challenges of the Christian life are different from day to day, year to year. If Christians are stuck in their relationship with God, they cannot point to a new spiritual learning or a new insight into the Christian life. Older parents who stop growing spiritually begin to feel the loss of their faith.

2. Is prayer important to you? Are you praying more or less? If one family member quits speaking to another, it is clearly the result of a breach—anger, hurt feelings, betrayal. If a Christian quits speaking to God, then often the same kind of emotions and forces are at work. Anger makes prayer difficult if a Christian is determined to only pray in sweet words and voices. Hurt feelings and betrayal may be equally hard to express. Prayer is a primary indicator of the condition of the relationship one has with God.

3. Are you telling other people about God's love? Christians with a healthy soul want others to have what they have. Witnessing for the healthy soul is almost an automatic response to someone else's need. When a Christian is in spiritual trouble, witnessing dies out.

Adult children will want to look for changes in spiritual habits and attitudes and open conversations if their older parents seem to be in need. Likewise, older parents can often, because of their experience, spot spiritual decline in their loved ones.

Hungry souls. When energy is taken up in trying to stay well, in watching a close budget, in losing friends to death and illness, older parents may become too wrapped up in these things to pay attention to their spirits. There are ways to feed the soul.

Meditation is one way. When many westerners hear the word "meditation," they think of Buddhists in saffron-colored robes. Meditation is simply the turning of one's attention to spiritual matters without the interruption or competition of noise and tasks. It can be simply lying on the sofa and listening to beautiful music for twenty minutes or reading a Scripture and repeating it over and over until all the words are a part of the heart. Meditation is an adult time-out. It is the chance to stop whatever is happening and catch one's breath and balance.

Using the senses is a way to feed the soul. Looking at family photos and taking in the beauty of all the faces of family and friends from over the years is one way of taking in through the eyes food for the soul. Beautiful art is another.

I admit it sounds silly, but I just sit and look at this book of great Impressionists. I feel so enriched by their beauty. It calms me and reminds me of the tremendous amount of creative power of human beings and how much of each person lives on after them.
　　　　　　　　　　　　　　　　　　　　　　　　—Julia

Getting one's hands in clay or listening to music will also feed one's spirit. Senses are an important way to receive information and therefore one pathway to the heart.

As the community of faith and larger community appreciate the spirituality and wisdom of older adults, the biggest challenge to their spiritual well-being may be the move from independent living into a nursing care environment.

A Word for the Faithful. All people need the opportunity to pass their experiences and knowledge on to others in order to contribute part of their lives to the larger world. Proverbs 2 is a beautiful text about wisdom as a gift from God:

> My child, if you accept my words
>> and treasure up my commandments within you,
> making your ear attentive to wisdom
>> and inclining your heart to understanding;
> if you indeed cry out for insight,
>> and raise your voice for understanding;
> if you seek it like silver,
>> and search for it as for hidden treasures—
> then you will understand the fear of the LORD
>> and find the knowledge of God.
> For the LORD gives wisdom;
>> from his mouth come knowledge and under-
>>> standing;
> he stores up sound wisdom for the upright;
>> he is a shield to those who walk blamelessly,
> guarding the paths of justice
>> and preserving the way of his faithful ones.
> Then you will understand righteousness and justice
>> and equity, every good path;
> for wisdom will come into your heart,
>> and knowledge will be pleasant to your soul;
> prudence will watch over you;
>> and understanding will guard you.
>> —Proverbs 2:1-11

If older adults are a source of wisdom, then they too are a gift from God.

A Prayer for Older Parents. Dear God, thank you for my whole life and all the times of love and hope, frustration and anger, celebration and grief that have filled my life. Help me to discover the wisdom I have to offer others and a way to tell my story to the world. Amen.

A Prayer for Adult Children of Older Parents. Dear God, help me to see my parents as beautiful sources of wisdom and spirituality. Give me the patience and discernment to truly hear their stories. Amen.

CHAPTER 6

WHEN IS HOME NOT ENOUGH?

My daughter and her husband have taken me to visit three or four nursing homes. They call them retirement centers or nursing care facilities. I know what they are. My daughter talks about the lovely sunshine coming in the window, the pretty curtains, and the good food. My son-in-law talks about the excellent care. I know they love me. But I see lots of old people, really old people, sitting, waiting to die. I smell urine and disinfectant and rotting bodies. People are decaying before they die. I see rooms with no locks and shared bathrooms. I see no room for my piano or my books. I see myself sitting, waiting to die. Jean says she'll visit often, but they forget. We all know that. It happened to Millie and Julia that way. They sat and waited to die. I used to teach children to read and I was important in their lives. Now all I am supposed to care about is pretty curtains. Pretty curtains are not enough.

—Agnes, 86

Agnes and her daughter, like many older parents and adult children, are in the same postretirement group. Her daughter, Jean, age sixty-five, has just completed thirty years of service in the U.S. Post Office and is ready to carry out all the travel plans she and her husband have made. Her mother, suffering from the early stages of senile dementia, seems to many people to be lucid and capable, though frail. Jean sees her mother almost every day and she knows that often her mother cannot remember what day it is or if she has eaten breakfast or taken her medication. Jean believes that her mother should not be alone, whether or not Jean is traveling out of town. Like most of the persons entering nursing care facilities, Agnes has lost some mental acuity and is physically frail. These persons are usually in the oldest population group.

Jean genuinely fears for her mother's life if Agnes continues to live alone, for if she takes more than the prescribed amount of heart medication, it can be dangerous. Twice her mother has forgotten to turn off the stove and almost started a fire. Jean wants to keep her mother alive as long as possible. She sees the nursing care facilities as a relief for the burden of cooking, shopping, cleaning, and paying bills for her mother.

Agnes does not so much fear for loss of life. She has, after all, buried a husband, a son, her own parents, three sisters, two brothers, and most of her friends. Agnes knows she will die. She fears indignity, loss of privacy, and loss of control of her life during the time she has remaining. Because Agnes is not always lucid, it is doubly hard for her to communicate these fears with Jean.

Agnes would rather risk having an accident or forgetting to turn off the stove than be in a nursing care facility. One man expressed his feelings about being allowed to take risks by reminding his children that every time they tried something new as children he feared for their safety. He let them take the risks they needed to take in order to grow and learn. He wants his children to let him take the risks he needs to take. "To risk," he said, "is to live, and to be alive one must take risks." For Agnes, death at eighty-seven in her home is preferable to death at ninety-three in a nursing home. She sees the nursing home as death; her daughter sees it as life.

GRIEFS AND FEARS

Parents who have reached an age and capacity where they can no longer live alone grieve the loss of personal control and familiar surroundings. They fear dying alone, forgotten, or living lives that are a burden to those they love. Older parents grieve the loss of physical and mental abilities and their change of status in society. They fear being shunned by others.

Adult children grieve the relationships they once had with their parents and the loss of parental care. They fear that their parents will suffer or that there will not be enough money to care for them. They grieve changes in the family and the loss of family traditions such as Thanksgiving Day at mother's house. And they fear growing old themselves, facing the same problems as their parents.

Often adult children carry a huge burden of guilt when it is necessary for parents to leave independent-living situations. Making the emotional transition is as important as finding the right care options. Older parents may react with depression, anger, frustration, aggression, hostility, and fear when they must leave their home. Some become withdrawn and even self-destructive. Adult children may take negative social behavior as personal attacks, while the parents feel as though they are fighting for survival. These fights often take place within the family, but many older adults fully realize that they are not fighting just their children but an entire social structure and the way it views aging.

Agnes, like many older adults, most of whom are women, has limited experience in asking directly for what she wants from authority figures or institutional personnel. Doctors and other medical workers have been held in awe and were to be absolutely obeyed; even asking a question is forbidden.

Many older parents have three real, and not unfounded, fears about giving up their independent living.

1. *Will I be able to get what I need?* Will I have to take part in events, go places, or eat things I don't like? Will they make

me share a room with someone I don't like? Many institutions allow residents to stay in their rooms if they do not want to participate, but have only one menu. If residents do not care for the food, they are offered a dietary supplement of some kind in place of it. Roommates are often assigned at first, but as time passes some changes are usually allowed to accommodate personal tastes. Adult children may want to ask these questions when considering any placement.

2. *What will I do if I hate it there?* If I give up my home, what will happen if I can't go back again? Will I have the chance to choose another place to live?

No one seems to understand why we all hate nursing homes. It's easy. No one ever gets better and goes home. No one leaves those places except to go to the cemetery. You don't get out alive.

—Ellie

Ellie is not completely right. For some older adults the decision to go into a nursing facility is permanent and they can't go home again, especially if they have a disease that is progressive. Their homes may be sold to finance their care, and unless they move to a different kind of care facility, as from intermediate to complete care, seldom are moves made because waiting lists are long on the better facilities. But many older adults are only in care facilities to have physical therapy or other rehabilitative medical care before they return to their homes. Each person is different.

3. *Will I see my family again?* Will they forget me? Will it be too much trouble for them to come to see me? Another part of this last fear has to with showing confusion and memory loss. Many older adults try to hide their physical symptoms for fear that if they cannot communicate, remember, and talk as they always have, their children and grandchildren will not want to be with them.

Women vary not only in their capacities for adjustment but also in their capacities as caregivers. Many women work, maintain a home, and care for children as they try also to care for their aging parents. They need to be able to admit, without being judged, that they cannot do more than they are doing or than they have already done toward their parents' care. The responsibility of caregivers can be a heavy load, especially if they must constantly try not to take over too much or seem too assertive.

The lines of what decisions an adult child can make are often fuzzy and difficult to define. Adult children need to know exactly what is expected of them by their parents and what their parents would see as interference. Are they to visit only? Are they to purchase clothing? Are they to take care of financial concerns?

I know that it's hard to be my daughter sometimes. I need her, but it hurts to take help. I hired someone to wash and iron the curtains last week and she was mad because she wanted to help. She said I should have saved my money. I said I wanted to be able to yell at the person helping in case they didn't do it right. She laughed so hard. She told me I'd yelled at her for years whenever I wanted, so why be shy now? She's right. I love it when we laugh together. She's going to come over next week and do the bedspreads.

—Barbara, 76, retired cook

Barbara and her daughter have found the gift of being honest with each other.

NURSING CARE

Two kinds of nursing care are available to older parents. One is in-home care and the other is a residential care situation in which the older parent moves into other housing. The first kind of care can be expensive if round-the-clock professional nurses are needed. It is less expensive if care is only needed for a few hours a day for medications and personal care needs. Limited resources to pay for this care and older persons having a hard time adjusting to strangers in their home represent the difficulties of this option. Adult children also carry a heavier load than before in trying to keep down the costs of in-home care. Older adults do better when allowed to do all they can for as long as they can. They also do better when they stay in familiar surroundings, in their own home, for as long as possible.

When care in their home or in one of their children's homes is impossible, older adults must receive residential care. Most persons moving into a residential care situation view this move as their last one. There are three basic levels of residential care, and some retirement centers offer the opportunity to move from one level to another within the same system. When older parents make the move to a residential institution, whatever the level of care, they look at the place they will be living and believe this is where they will die. The reality is that at any given time only about 5 percent of older people are in nursing homes on a long-term basis. During a year another 4 percent are in a nursing home for a shorter period of time, usually moving from home to hospital to nursing home and back to home. The fear of nursing homes does not come from the statistics about the number of people who eventually live there but from deeply ingrained ideas about what happens there.

While residential care facilities are not "snake pits" of filth and unpleasantness as they were once imagined, they are still not home. Adult children work hard to secure a place in a clean, pleasant, well-staffed, safe place for their parents. However, the older parents moving there realize they have relinquished that most basic of all freedoms, the freedom to move to another place if they do not like the one they are in. These restrictions, combined with the medical and physical needs that forced them to give up independent living, make the adjustment to such living difficult.

Another perception of nursing care facilities is that they are regimented and residents must obey a flurry of rules. Most older parents have limited personal experience as a patient in nursing care facilities. They do have experience in hospitals and so transfer the hospital experience—regular checks of blood pressure and temperature, lights out at a certain time—to what they perceive a nursing care environment will involve. The amount of regimentation and personal choices greatly vary from one care situation to another. For many older parents almost any alternative seems preferable, at least in thinking about it. The reality is often that residential care is often the best overall solution for frail elderly persons or persons with moderate to later stages of senile dementia.

Symbolism. One adjustment to nursing care is the change from independent to dependent living. This move from independence to dependence has come to symbolize a return to childhood or childlike relationships. This is not true, but the image lingers on in this culture. People are heard to say things such as "She's in her second childhood" and "His mind is like a child's." The truth is that mentally and physically impaired older parents suffer a tremendous loss because they were once independent. Children are dependent but looking toward independence; older parents were independent but looking toward dependence for the rest of their lives. Older parents possess wisdom and knowledge that children do not have, even if in the last stages of Alzheimer's disease they may not be able to express it or be aware of it. Children have energy and innocence; older parents have experience and history.

The comparison of older parents to children is also negative for their adult children, who are patient and understanding with their own children and then are surprised at the feelings of rebellion and impatience they have in connection with dependent parents. The difference is in that children are supposed to be dependent and adults are equipped, in most cases, to deal with this dependence. They know this dependence is temporary and have joy in seeing the growth and development of their children. Dependence from older parents is longer term, only ending with death. Adult children who continue to see their parents as adults and to respect them as parents are better able to put the dependence in perspective.

Older parents who must receive nursing care to survive deserve to be treated like adults who have become dependent and not like children. To be treated like an adult with specific needs and abilities, however limited, is to feel like a part of the community. Some older parents become angry when talked to as if they are children or when their children overexplain things as if they could not understand their surroundings. There are great personal rewards for adult children who resist the temptation to do this and instead treat their dependent parents like adults with special needs.

My mother has had a broken pelvis and a broken hip. She is so frail, but she is so sharp. She is incontinent, but it is embarrassing for her to have to wear a diaper. At first I let her embarrassment influence me, and cleaning and bathing her was something I dreaded. Then I decided to use the time to have her tell me stories of when she was young. I pretended the cleaning and bathing were just routine, almost as if it weren't happening, and concentrated on her memories. I actually began to look forward to these times.
—Stephanie, 62, daughter of Violet, 84, retired homemaker

Nothing can completely diminish the loss of privacy and self-esteem that comes with being dependent on others, but being treated as an adult helps soften the blow.

Redefinition of self. Moving into a nursing care facility, perhaps more than any other event in aging, forces older parents to redefine who they are because their relationship to their family, friends, and culture has changed radically.

Shortly after my father's death I asked my mother what she was doing to keep busy. She said she was driving the "old widow women" in her church back and forth to services. "What are you?" I asked her. "I'm not old yet; they are in the nursing home." I guess when I was ten, forty was old. Now that I'm forty, seventy is old. For my mother who is seventy, ninety is old. She

wants to go to the same nursing home when she gets old. She would rather die first, but if she doesn't, she wants to go to that nursing home. Death is preferable to a nursing home, and the nursing home to being a burden on her children.
—Martha, 40, daughter of Daisy, 70

Nursing home care is a clear indicator that someone is old. At this point self-esteem becomes a major issue. The self-esteem of older parents sustains a blow from having to redefine themselves as dependent. The self-esteem of their adult children often suffers because they have unrealistic expectations of themselves and their ability to care for their parents.

Control. The highest need for those persons entering a nursing care environment is for choices and control in their lives. This need for autonomy may be different for men and women. More than 70 percent of the residents of nursing homes are women; 80 percent of these are over the age of seventy-five (Brody and Semel 1993, 40). Women who have traditionally been in caregiving roles may find the adjustment to being cared for particularly difficult. Men may find that living by rules and schedules set by someone else is the most difficult adjustment.

Some older adults rebel by ceasing to eat. Others refuse to participate in group activities, while others refuse to form new relationships. They seem to be stubbornly sabotaging efforts to make their life better. What may really be happening is that the ability to say no is the only power they still have.

Choices give more control. Whatever care environment the older person is in, home or assisted living or nursing care facility, the presence of choices is essential. With the exception of severe cases of Alzheimer's disease or extreme physical problems that limit communications, such as a paralyzing stroke, most older parents are able to make their wishes known right up until the time of their death. Choosing when to eat and when to sleep, what to wear, what music or television program to enjoy—all of these choices can offer more control to older parents.

It seems to me to be a basic right—to say, "I don't want to shave today." Good grief! I'm ninety-two years old. Why should I shave every day? God loves me with my whiskers showing. And why do I need to wear slippers? I like to go barefoot. I've gone barefoot most of my life. Is it too much to ask to go barefoot in my own bedroom? When did my feet become my daughter's business?
—Herman, 92, retired carpenter

Timing. Some older parents, such as Daisy, understand clearly that the time may come for them to move into a nursing home, and when it does, they will go to live in the facility of their choice. Some older parents find it easier to go to a nursing home from a hospital rather than from home. Hospital social service workers can often help in the transition by counseling with older parents.

As hard as it is, adult children may need to let their older parents have one fall or accident so that they themselves make the decision that more supervised living is needed. The move may be later than the children would want and somewhat earlier than the parent would want. Families are able to give different levels of support and help to older parents as they progress in their loss of mental acuity and increase in physical frailty at different rates.

Family physicians who look after the health of both members of an older couple often will make recommendations. Sometimes residential care is needed for the more frail person in the couple in order to allow the spouse to stay healthier longer.

FAITH, PROMISES, AND SEARCHING FOR WAYS TO HONOR

Many young men and women promise themselves and their parents that there will be no nursing home for the parents. Over and over again this promise has to be broken by the practical demands of life. There is also the commandment that children learn at an early age: "Honor your father and your mother, so that your days may be long in the land that the LORD your God is giving you" (Exodus 20:12). What does it mean to honor one's mother and father in the face of debilitating illness?

Convenience or quality of care. There exists a stereotype of the modern family in which Grandma and Grandpa are tucked away in a nursing home so that the family is free to have a care-free social life and travel without the worry of care for aging parents. This is seldom true. This stereotype has led some older parents to fail to consider the real reason most families feel forced to consider nursing home facilities—the quality of care. Many diseases require a carefully monitored balance of medication, and the inability to walk or take care of personal hygiene often means a full-time presence is needed to be sure older parents are cared for safely.

Honoring one's parents certainly means seeing that they are physically safe when they are no longer able to ensure their own safety. It also means allowing them to decide for themselves, as much as possible, the kind of care they receive and from whom. The tension becomes almost unbearable when the older parents do not want to accept the care their adult children think they need.

There are some elements of faith life that are important at any level of tension, compromise, and change.

Honesty honors both children and parents. As hard as it is to say clearly things that one knows will cause pain, it is the honorable action.

I finally said to Mother, "There are no more choices that will allow you to live at home, because you cannot walk alone and we cannot afford twenty-four-hour nursing care except as a part of a larger group setting. We love you, and we wish you could be young forever. But you can't, and we can't change what is happening to you. You can choose the facility you want to live in,

you can choose what to do with you home and possessions, but
you can't choose to live alone."

—John, 54, son of Laurie, 86

Laurie had already broken one hip. She was mentally alert
and her usual bright self, but her physical abilities were
beyond living alone. It would be cruel to pretend otherwise.

I know that I have to make this adjustment, and that I have to
be here. I hate that I can't do what I used to do. I hate it! I hate
it! But my son said that he had no other choice and that I had
no other choice. Pretending I was still sixty years old wouldn't
help. I've been through a lot in my life, but this is the worst.

—Laurie, 86, homemaker

Another element of all conversations between adult children and elderly parents is appreciation. Whatever feelings
adult children might have about their upbringing and short-
comings they perceive in their parents' lives, this is not the
time for those issues to be the central focus. Most children,
unless they are survivors of abuse of some kind, can be sin-
cerely thankful for the contribution their parents have made to
their lives. Genuine thanksgiving helps ease painful moments
and is always a part of honoring one's parents.

A third element of honoring one's parents is respect of personal privacy and integrity of their bodies. Because adult children have developed paternal and maternal instincts toward
their own children, it is easy to slip into treating their parents
like children—in helping them dress and undress, telling them
when to eat and what to eat, and so on. Elderly parents are often
embarrassed by their children's attempts to help them with
dressing and bathroom needs and prefer help from strangers
instead.

I'm eighty-seven years old, and my children have decided that
when they are here they'll clean out my refrigerator and bring gro-
ceries—usually things I don't eat—and put them in the cabinets

for me. Then, the other day, my daughter told me that she had been looking at my underwear and some of it needed to be replaced. Imagine, going through my drawers. I told her to get out of my house until she could show some respect. She said if I couldn't accept a little help, then it would be a cold day in hell before she tried to help me again. It was really awful. I want my daughter to come see me, and I could use some help with the house and food, but going through my drawers was the last straw.

—Agnes

Agnes's daughter was trying to help, but her approach felt intrusive to Agnes. A better approach would be for her to ask Agnes for a list of the groceries she wants and to tell Agnes that if she needs clothes she would like to help her. Agnes could then decide what she needs, and if her underwear doesn't meet her daughter's standards, then what would be more important— letting Agnes retain her dignity and wear worn underwear or have Agnes wear good underwear but feel like her daughter doesn't respect her.

Older children are not alone. The community of faith has a responsibility to see that adult children of older parents know they are not the only people concerned about or responsible for their parents' care. The Scriptures command the entire community of faith, everyone in Christ's body, to care for widows and orphans and those infirm and unable to care for themselves. The problem is also a problem of society in general, not just the churches and families.

My Sunday school teacher drives me to the doctor once a month because my son and daughter-in-law work. My pastor comes and gets me and takes me to lunch now and then. I have a list of people to call if something happens during the day when I'm home alone. Living with my daughter is intense at times, and we have our little spats, but it is easier because other people care for me. I know that I'll need to go to the home [meaning the local nursing care facility] soon because I'm getting weaker and it's hard

*for me to walk. I dread that, but I know there will still be people
who come to see me and visit. That helps.*
                              —Esther, 89, retired homemaker

Part of the pressure on families is the decision of many
church communities not to be as involved in the lives of individual church members. Ministers are often encouraged to keep
a "professional" distance, and churches' monetary aid to older
members is limited to occasional emergency gifts. In the name
of not interfering and as a response to ever-growing responsibilities of their own, some churches have made aging the problem
of the individual family, not of the faith community.

Most communities of faith and their leaders are struggling
with how to help aging parishioners and their families. Even
though ministries within the nursing home are somewhat limited to worship services and visits, there are many ways in
which the church can be involved before the move to the nursing home is made and in using its power to demand better care
in nursing facilities. Not only can church members participate
in a personal ministry to persons in nursing homes, but they
can be advocates for better care facilities through legal and
social systems.

LEVELS OF CARE

Whether an elderly person is at home or in a nursing care
facility, different levels of care are needed.

Helpful environment. A helpful environment might include
an apartment or room in enriched housing that gives older parents the chance to live together in a community and seek the
amount of help they need to thrive. One such program has older
parents sharing an apartment with housekeeping support and
cooking seven days a week.

Older parents often have their needs met by a community
outside of their children and grandchildren. Often older adults
who are able to drive take those who are not still driving to

church or shopping. They may be paid back with freshly baked bread or help of some other kind. This community is satisfying for older parents because they give as well as receive. Adult children who are able to find ways to continue to receive from their older parents help the family maintain the healthy balance of helping one another.

Partial care. A partial care environment is one that provides medical care as needed and some care such as housekeeping and cooking. Some retirement centers give residents a choice of small apartments, rooms, or nursing facilities as they are needed. It is critical that older adults be allowed to do as much for themselves and make as many decisions for themselves as they can.

Complete care. A total care environment refers to the complete physical care of residents. Sometimes people in this environment are called patients because of the level of care. Becoming a "patient" rather than a "resident" is still another adjustment in self-esteem and self-definition. When complete care is needed in a private home, older parents must adjust to an influx of strangers into the home, a necessary invasion of privacy. Some report feelings of being watched or that the house is no long their own.

Some older parents are asked to live in their children's homes. In some instances this works well as a helpful environment, in others it does not work well at all. In considering having older parents move into their children's homes, both parents and children may want to ask these questions:

1. *Is there some private space for everyone?* An older parent relegated to a daybed in the den will probably not be as happy as one who has his or her own room. If all the bedrooms are upstairs and the older parent cannot negotiate the stairs, then making the den into a private bedroom is the best option. Likewise, the adult children and their children need private space.

2. *Are there some guidelines for communal space?* Teenagers wanting to watch music videos round-the-clock might clash with Grandfather watching his favorite show. Obviously, everyone has to make compromises, but have all family members understood and agreed to compromise? Sometimes an investment in earphones and an additional television can solve the problem; other times everyone has to decide that living together requires giving up and giving in.

3. *What are the expectations?* Are the older parents expected to turn over all or part of their retirement checks to help with the expenses? Do adult children expect some work from adult parents? One family reported that mother and daughter argued constantly over little things. The trouble turned out to be the stove. Mother kept cleaning it in an effort to help her daughter, but the daughter saw this as a criticism of her housekeeping. What are the limitations? If Father has moved in because he has gotten forgetful about his medicine, then will his daughter give him the medicines each morning or will he continue to take them himself? Often the levels of contribution become unbalanced when either adult children or older parents try to do everything.

4. *Can we accept our differences?* Whether or not to put raisins in cinnamon buns may not seem like much, but it can lead to hours, even days, of hurt feelings if the people sharing the kitchen cannot agree to be different. There are also big differences that create conflict, such as changes in the ways grandchildren are disciplined or the dating habits of teenagers. The temptation of older parents to try to raise their grandchildren is usually significant, and the temptation of adult children to try to change the things about their parents that have always irritated them is strong. Often to agree to disagree brings peace more quickly than trying to come to agreement.

Care questions. Some basic questions must be resolved in either in-home care situations or residential institutions.

In-home care providers are usually supplied or recommended by health-care agencies. However, the day-to-day supervision of these care providers is often the job of a spouse or adult child. Some things to get straight from the beginning are:

1. *Who provides baths and personal health care?* Unfortunately, some health-care workers do not wish to bathe patients. One older man preferred to bathe at night, but his wife found that worker after worker told her they had chosen the night shift so that they wouldn't have to bathe patients. Because usually more than one person will be providing care, these workers should know from the beginning exactly what they are to do on each shift.

2. *Who keeps track of medicines and the need for refills?* If one worker is a nurse and the other a housekeeping aide, then the decision is easy. If all the workers are nurses, or none are, this must be outlined.

3. *What housekeeping and cooking is expected?* One home health aide cleaned the oven when she cleaned the kitchen after preparing lunch; another did not set foot in the kitchen except to get herself a snack. Divisions of labor must be communicated. Not only do the workers need to know what to do but what not to do. The health aide that cleaned the oven was fired for interfering with the cook's work because the cook did not like the way the oven was cleaned. The one who only went to the kitchen to eat was fired for not feeding her patient.

4. *What about holidays and other special times?* An older woman reports hating Christmas because she has to bathe and care for her husband and she is so fearful she will drop him. The home health aide demanded double pay for holidays, and the woman did not know if she could afford it. These arrangements should all be discussed in advance.

Additional supervisory problems may include language and attentiveness. Some health-care aides are verbally abusive to uncooperative patients or inattentive to quiet patients who are unable to make many demands or who sleep a great deal of the time. This small minority of aides give many hardworking and caring workers a difficult reputation to overcome. Adult children might want to surprise aides in the times and frequency of their visits until they are satisfied with the compassion and ability of the people they have hired to care for their older parents.

Institutional questions are similar. Here are some questions both older parents and their adult children might want to ask of a nursing facility:

1. *How are medical needs met?* Are personal physicians called? Does the facility have its own physician on call? Who makes decisions about when to call a physician? Who decides when an illness warrants calling the adult children of a resident?

2. *What are the dietary arrangements?* Do the residents have a choice of foods? Can they eat between meals or off hours if they are hungry? How are the special needs of diabetics and others met?

3. *Who monitors residents' needs?* Are there patient advocates who regularly inquire about residents' satisfaction?

4. *Are personal items allowed?* Often even the smallest of personal items can help the transition to a full-care facility. Can residents have their own quilts and pillows? Can they have a television in their room and pictures of their families on the walls?

5. *How are room assignments made?* Can residents have private rooms? Can residents change rooms if they are unhappy with their roommates?

6. *What resident services are offered?* Laundry? Dry cleaning? Beauty and barber shops? Activities such as movies or field trips? Is there opportunity for fresh air and time out-of-doors?

7. *Who is in charge?* Both older parents and family members need to know to whom they can make complaints and requests and the process for resolving problems.

The reality is that usually there are only a few choices for residential care and a waiting list for the best of those choices. Some older parents choose to get on the waiting list of their chosen place long before they believe they'll need it. Adult children might begin looking at possibilities before the time when they are urgently needed.

GETTING WHAT WE NEED

Aging does not change basic needs. Maslow's Hierarchy of Needs has long been used by health-care professionals to look at the human experience. Age does not diminish the basic needs of humans: physical needs (shelter, warmth, food), emotional needs (love, being loved, being needed), and spiritual needs (a belief in a higher power, hope, faith). Getting basic needs met often takes all the energy older parents have.

A nursing home facility is first and foremost a place where both biological needs and safety and security needs are met. It is also a community where belonging, self-esteem, and fulfillment of some dreams or goals can be possible in differing degrees as the abilities of residents permit. Sometimes the small things can meet large needs. It can be hard for residents to find a way to ask for what they need. One counselor told of a resident who wanted a cup of yogurt but did not even consider asking for it. She did not know she could make requests and felt totally under the control of the institutional caregivers. After much encouragement, she asked for the yogurt and got it to her surprise (Brody and Semel 1993, 20).

To adult children this may seem simple, but it is important that older parents feel free to ask for what they need and want and to have those requests taken seriously.

Adult children's needs must be considered, too. They have the same order of needs as their older parents and must be free to try to get their needs met.

My mother asks more and more of me. Nothing is enough. I can't do it anymore and I don't know what to do. I see her and know how much I love her and want to care for her. I can't do what she wants me to. When do I get to sleep?
                            —Joy, 45, daughter of Eleanor, 76

When enough is enough, adult children must ask for help, and they deserve the support of their community to do the best possible thing for themselves and their parents.

The time will come in the family's life when one parent dies and the family shifts again. The next chapter looks at this initial grief process and the family.

A Word for the Faithful. Honoring one's parents has to do with honesty, respect, and gratitude as well as seeing that parents have the best care possible given all the elements that must be considered. It is a hard time for persons and relationships that can be made easier by the support of the rest of the faith community.

A Prayer for Older Parents. Dear God, you've been faithful to me throughout my life and the struggles and changes I have had to face. Please be with me now and show me how to be honest with my children about my feelings and needs. Give me patience, grace, and faith. Amen.

A Prayer for Adult Children of Older Parents. Dear God, help me to be honest with my parents about the hard decisions facing them. Show me how to be full of gratitude and respect. Please be with my parents now and make them feel loved and wanted wherever they are. Amen.

CHAPTER 7

WHEN THE FIRST PARENT DIES

I have wondered why I would have such a horrible thing as liver cancer and why I would have to die now. I know I am old and I know that my children are grown. I want to live, but I can't. I know that. I have so much to say to my children. I want them to know what it is like to wake up in the morning and wonder, Will this be the day that I die? I want them to know that I am not afraid, only sad. I spent much of my life teaching these children how to live. They are grown with children of their own, but I still see them as my own little darlings. I guess now I must teach them how to die. I pray for grace, dignity, and humor. I want to go laughing. I want to meet my God with a smile. How do I begin to tell them? They cry when I even mention it. I could never bear to see them cry.

—Amanda, 84, homemaker, upon learning of her cancer

Older parents must face their own mortality and often have a need to discuss their coming death—whether many years away or imminent—with their adult children. On the other hand, the children may be avoiding their parents' mortality and do not want to discuss their death. The first death of a parent is a loss of opportunity for resolution of issues in that relationship. It also changes the relationship adult children have with their surviving parent.

All of the missed opportunities for communication and compassion become obvious to some adult children, who then try to take advantage of remaining time with their surviving parent. For others the idea of losing a second parent to death is so devastating that they withdraw from forming a closer relationship with the surviving parent. The family history and individual personalities are important elements in the mix. Death changes those who are left alive, though, and there are some common elements for every family.

FIRST PARENT DEATH

The vast majority of older parents have adjusted throughout their lives to the changes in their family. Many have known or suspected for some time that their next adjustment would be to the death of their spouse. The expectation of this culture, based on experience, is that a woman will live longer than her husband and that she will give him care in his last illness. Obviously this is not always true. When it is not, the death of a wife can be particularly heartbreaking to the surviving husband who never thought he would face this loss. While women have learned to visualize the loss of their husband to death and begin to plan how to survive it, men often have not.

Gender differences are important. One researcher reports that men see death as an antagonist, an enemy; women see death as merciful (Waters and Goodman 1990, 142). Perhaps this is because women live longer and face longer periods of debilitation from which death is a release. Perhaps the traditional role of women as caregivers to dying persons gives them a different perspective because of the pain and discomfort they see. Irregardless of which parent is the first to die, the surviving parent, as well as the adult children, will face a grief process that is common to most persons.

When dying begins. Because of the expectation of death in old age, in some ways dying begins when older parents recognize and accept the inevitable aging process. More specifically, many people believe that dying begins when one learns that his or her last illness is in progress.

Knowing you are going to die is different than knowing how you are going to die. It changes the way you look upon death when you can name the disease that will be your end. Most days my cancer is an enemy of the first order because it will take me from my loved ones. But as I have gotten sicker, there are days when it is almost a friend, pushing me gently toward another shore, another world. I guess if I didn't believe in an afterlife, it would be impossible to face this cancer. I do believe. I know my parents are waiting for me. I miss them sometimes. I want every minute of life in this world that I can have, but I am dying and the next world is waiting.

—Amanda, two months into her illness

Some older parents have said that dying, for them, began when they had to tell the ones they loved that they were dying. Others say it began when they could no longer live the life they had always lived. Others say it begins when the last days of the illness make this world uncomfortable and the next world welcoming.

Almost all older parents have a greater fear of their last illness and its discomfort and of how they will die than of death itself. This is true of both those who believe in an afterlife and those who do not. However, beliefs about death influence the grief process.

Beliefs about death. Those who live with the promise of eternal life through the grace and love of Jesus Christ often talk about their loved one in terms of his or her being in heaven or paradise. This most basic Christian belief provides much comfort for older adults. Those who do not believe in a life after death often talk about death in terms of their loved one being free from pain and at eternal rest. For both groups, the cessation of pain for the loved one seems to be a source of comfort and those who are in pain may look forward to death rather than dread it.

The beliefs of adult children may differ from that of their surviving parent, and even their desires concerning funeral arrangements and last goodbyes may be different. There is an unspoken hierarchy that says the spouse's desires rule. However, adult children should also have the chance to speak up and make suggestions. The grief of adult children and grandchildren can get lost in their concern for the surviving parent. It is often the surviving parent, acting as a parent, that brings the adult children's grief into the center of attention and allows them to express their grief. No one's grief is more or less important than anyone else's. Everyone deserves to have his or her grief recognized by the whole group.

My son does not believe in cremation, although that is what my husband wanted. We talked before he died, and he agreed to let my son bury him instead. He said, "I'll be gone. Do what he wants." Even in death my husband was looking out for his family. He never failed to think of us. He never failed to think of me. Until now I hadn't realized what it meant to be first in someone's life. I'll miss that. I'll miss knowing that I am absolutely loved.
—Mildred, 84, widow of Oscar

Word of warning: Most adult children who have had difficult or painfully unsettled relationships with a parent find the loss of that parent much harder to bear than the loss of a parent with whom a close and rewarding relationship was maintained. The unresolved issues, including guilt, make the grief all the worse.

New needs. The surviving parent will experience new needs for physical attention and his or her children will want to find ways to help meet these needs.

After he came home from World War II, we were never separated for more than a few days at a time when one of the girls had a

baby and I would go to be with her. We were together all the time
for almost fifty years. At night, long after he was too sick for us
to have sex, we would fall asleep holding hands. Sometimes in
the night one of us would wake up and just reach over and touch
the other one. I'll miss having his hand to hold.

—Mildred

There is no way for adult children to fill such a void. It would
be frustrating and self-defeating to try. However, Mildred's adult
children may want to be sure that sometimes she has a hand to
hold. The cultural idea of older persons is that they are past
physical and sexual contact. This is not true. Older parents are
often more open to signs of affection than other age groups
because they are less inhibited. Perhaps this is because they
have years of experience and wisdom and have learned for
themselves the importance of positive touch.

Consider also what the deceased spouse did for the surviving parent. Most couples develop a way of helping each other
over the years. Did the parent who died keep the checkbook
and finances? Then someone may need to step in and help the
other parent learn to do this. Did the parent who died do all the
driving? Is the surviving parent afraid or unable to drive?
Perhaps a regularly scheduled trip for shopping is needed. Did
the parent who died keep track of the couple's medicine? How
can this be done by an adult child?

The best way to answer these questions is for the adult children to simply ask what they need to do for their surviving parent. Asking for help is not easy for everyone, but accepting
offered help may be more comfortable.

GRIEVING

For many cultural reasons, the death of an older person is
often more accepted than the death of a young person, for older
persons are seen as having lived a long, full life with the chance
to make dreams come true. After a long illness, the death of an

older person is often seen as a relief and maybe even a form of healing. When a young person dies, the death is considered premature; the deceased was cheated out of a complete life.

If the person who dies is loved, there will be grief no matter what the age. The loss of a husband of fifty-eight years can be almost unbearable. Adult children also experience grief. No two people move through the cycles of grief exactly alike or with the same timing. It is important for both the surviving parent and the adult children to give each other room to be different.

Everyone grieves. As obvious as the statement "everyone grieves" seems, those who are grieving sometimes suspect that they are alone in their feelings. It is common for people to think there is something wrong with them if they have several days of depression and sadness or if they burst into tears unexpectedly. Grief is a sign of mental health. It is the natural reaction to loss.

Grief, like birth and death, is an essential part of the human experience. It is not a disease or mental illness to be cured. Grief is founded in attachment and separation. Humans become attached to one another, and within marriages and families these attachments are deep and meaningful. The separation of death and the pain of such separation is obviously a direct outgrowth of attachment. The memories grieving persons have of their loved ones are a touchstone or road mark that allow them to rebuild their sense of self in relation to the lost loved one. For example, after fifty-eight years of marriage Hilda's husband dies. She has a vivid image in her mind of him curled and frail in his hospital as the doctor pronounced him dead. This image fades as grief continues and she also has images of their getting married, of the two of them with their first child on Christmas morning, and literally thousands of other images that confirm for her that he did live, that they did love, and that he is gone. The more she remembers, the more confident she becomes in her knowledge of who he was to her and who she was to him. She then begins to add memories of her at his funeral, sorting his clothing, and learning to be without him. Through this process she redefines herself as a widow instead of a wife and begins to feel whole again. The memories help her to reaffirm who she is.

Grief is a composite of many emotions. Elisabeth Kübler-Ross outlined stages of acceptance of terminal illness in her landmark book, *On Death and Dying*, but these are not the same as the stages of grief. Grief seems to be cyclical. Grieving persons may go through a long and painful cycle of sadness only to find that sadness has returned, less intensely perhaps, several months later. Some counselors have felt that because the movements between the emotions in grief can be rapid that there are no distinct stages (MacDonald 1993). Instead, grief might be better understood by looking at a variety of possible emotions and responses.

Denial, numbness, relief. Although many deaths of older persons are somewhat expected, the first reaction is still numbness or denial. There is an element of disbelief. Many recent widows and widowers talk about this feeling in terms of expecting the loved one to walk through the door or of having no memory of some period of time just after the death. Sometimes this is expressed as a loss of being in touch with others. The surviving parent may become reclusive or seemingly caught up in some fantasy life about a different time before the death of his or her spouse.

Adult children will have some of the same feelings, though perhaps with less intensity or for a shorter period of time. They may also worry about their surviving parent not being fully grounded in reality. It is true that a prolonged sense of denial might require an intervention by a counselor, but usually the "unrealness" of the death will pass fairly quickly. The surviving parent then begins to experience feelings of intense loss.

Extreme loss. Unless one has felt such intense loss, it is hard to explain, except to say there is a constant overwhelming sense of having part of oneself missing. This is often expressed in sadness and feelings of being torn apart or empty. These feelings of extreme loss are especially cyclical because they continue to recur throughout the grief process and throughout the rest of the surviving spouse's life. This feeling of emptiness is not only spiritual and emotional but physical. The sight of an empty chair in the living room or the smell of a favorite food of the deceased can bring it to the surface. Every sense brings in the message that the loved one is gone.

It took me a couple of days to figure it out. I couldn't eat breakfast at all, and then I realized that I couldn't eat because his chair was empty. To be closer to him, I began sitting in his chair. Then I could eat. It feels silly now, but at first it was the only way I could get toast and coffee down.

—Mildred

Mildred might feel as though she is doing fine for several weeks and then suddenly see an advertisement for her husband's favorite television show and be sad and lonely for days. The quickly changing emotions and the way the emotions come back make grief unpredictable.

Anger. Another common emotion is anger—deep, hateful, and painful. Sometimes the anger is directed toward the deceased person. It is not logical but it is common. The person who died "abandoned" his or her spouse and family. The fact that he or she did not choose to die or want to die is little comfort. The person has gone, and those left behind are angry.

The deceased person is not there to receive this anger so the people around the grieving family receive it. A surviving parent may lash out at the adult children, or the children, in turn, may lash out at the parent, especially if the deceased seems to be a larger loss than the death of the surviving parent would have been. Those who have heard their children say, "I wish you had died instead" are often able to understand this, just as their adult children are able to receive and understand their anger.

It is important to not let words said in misdirected anger continue to affect the family. A guideline for anger in grief management is that family members should be seen as whole people, not judged on just one moment of anger.

Anger is also expressed toward doctors and health-care workers, toward clergy persons and counselors, and toward God. Anger, like sadness, can leave and return again and again as the grief cycles continue.

Guilt. Guilt comes in when spouses and children have feelings of failure in connection with their loved ones. "If only I . . ." seems to be a hallmark of this part of the grief cycle. This may be guilt about something the grieving family member believes he or she should have done or said or should not have done or said.

I said when Dad died that I wish I had spent more time with him alone. Family time after I became an adult was always group time. We had so many people. My brothers, sisters, and I, with our children and grandchildren, now number forty-three people, and we would always come home on holidays. I won't do that with Mama. I'm going to come home in the middle of the year for no reason and just talk to her, be with her.
—Letha, 60, daughter of Mildred and Oscar

Guilt may be less specific, such as that an adult child was not a "good" daughter or son or that somehow if a different doctor or hospital had been found the parent might still be alive. Surviving spouses may feel they have somehow caused the last illness or failed to get the attention needed. They may also relive all the mistakes they made in the marriage, all the big and little hurts, and torture themselves with unreasonable guilt.

Adult children might sense that their surviving parent's guilt is overwhelming and need to counter that guilt with reality. They may want to remind their parent that the other parent did not hold a grudge, had forgiven them, or would not want them to feel badly.

Reliving the last days. One common activity of surviving spouses is reliving the last days of their spouse's life. They will recite to anyone who listens the stories of the last hours, the illness, the doctors, the nurses, and all the events. Each moment takes on importance, and the retelling of the story imprints the moments on the surviving spouse's memory.

Adult children can find this reliving painful at first and then irritating. Their ability to remember each moment may be greater than that of their surviving parent and their need to remember each moment may be less. But it is important for the process of remembering, because it is in remembering that healing and wholeness take place. Adult children may want to add other memories to these and help their parent move toward remembering an entire life.

Remembering an entire life. Death is most immediately the loss of relationship. By remembering the life of a loved one, surviving family members begin to develop a new form of relationship. This relationship is formed as a new self emerges for the grieving person. As the surviving parent and adult children face a future without the deceased parent, they must deal with separation. Through memories they reattach themselves to the deceased person in a new way. The parameters of this attachment, in its healthy form, are determined by the memories of the life once lived together.

In its unhealthy form, some loved ones seek to reattach themselves by communication with a spirit world or obsessive attachment to a certain object or place. A famous example is Mrs. Harry Houdini, who sought through mediums and psychics to contact her dead husband throughout the remainder of her life.

To reattach does not mean the end of grief. The cycles of sadness, anger, and guilt may continue for many years but in shorter duration and with less intensity. Because the physical person of the deceased can never be brought back, the loss is never completely forgotten.

FAITH AND LOSS

There is a deep and profound belief that most Christians share in a positive, benevolent life after death. This life after death is the promise of Christ to believers and the primary source of comfort for many Christians in times of loss. Reunion in the future that will be permanent is an image to which Christians cling.

For elderly parents there is also reunion in death. While adult children look toward reunion with their parents some day, this is the reunion that their elderly parents experience in death. Many ill and dying persons talk about their parents and their childhood. For many who are facing death, great comfort is taken in the reunion that is to come. For the very elderly, many friends, colleagues, and perhaps some children or grand-children are also waiting in eternity.

While clinging to this coming reunion eases grief, it does not relieve it completely. Death is loss, and surviving parents may find the intense loneliness and momentous changes almost too much to bear.

Adult children have the dual burden of dealing with their own grief as well as helping their surviving parent to deal with grief. This parent may become more and more dependent or demanding or may withdraw and become uncommunicative. For many, it is the first time in their lives that they have been alone.

I went from my father's house to my marriage. We had children very quickly, and by the time the children had all left home, we had a grandchild to raise. In my entire life I have never lived alone. I have been alone while my husband traveled, but I have never lived alone, day after day. I am surprised now by how quiet the house is. I can hear the clock ticking in the other room. I am surprised by how long the evenings are. The days are busy and full of housework, so they pass quickly, but I sit and wait for time to go to bed. I am lonely. I have never been lonely before. I mark

the calendar when I call my children so I don't call too often. I make a point of not bothering other people in the evening, because they have families. I try to find things to fill my time. It is a dreadful feeling, and I never knew how hard it was.
—Ruth, 74, homemaker

For Ruth, the church will make a big difference. She has found two different small groups to attend, one is a Bible study and one a quilting group. Because she can still drive, she has joined a group that provides transportation to doctors and hospitals.

I still have a hard time some evenings. My pastor has given each senior a "partner," and we call and talk to each other. She [the pastor] also calls me in the evening now and then just to see how I'm doing. When I'm lonely now I think that maybe someone will call, or I plan tomorrow's work. I'm still lonely sometimes, but it is not as bad.
—Ruth, several months later

One of the worst problems facing surviving partners is loneliness, and one of the biggest challenges facing the church is how to use the gifts of older parents and alleviate some of the loneliness. The obvious answers helped Ruth, but there are still those times when all the activities, telephone calls, and support cannot cut through the pain. Sometimes the only answer is just to hold someone's hand and let the tears flow. This grief is seen throughout the Scriptures and especially in the story of King David, who gave words to his grief in the psalms.

> As a deer longs for flowing streams,
>   so my soul longs for thee, O God.
> My soul thirsts for God,
>   for the living God.
> When shall I come and behold
>   the face of God?
> My tears have been my food
>   day and night,
> while men say to me continually,
>   "Where is your God?"

These things I remember,
    as I pour out my soul:
how I went with the throng,
    and led them in procession to the house of God,
with glad shouts and songs of thanksgiving,
    a multitude keeping festival.
Why are you cast down, O my soul,
    and why are you disquieted within me?
Hope in God; for I shall again praise him,
    my help and my God.

—Psalm 42:1-6

TALKING TO CHILDREN

A child's first experience with death is often the death of a grandparent or great-grandparent. It can be difficult explaining this loss to children, whose idea of death may come from a cartoon or video game where the destroyed character comes back to life again and again. The grandparent will not.

1. *Tell the truth.* Children can often sense when someone is lying to them even if they do not know exactly what the lie is. Death is when the physical body of someone quits working and living. The family beliefs about life after death, the spirit, and the soul should be communicated, too. Promises of heaven are valuable, but it should be made clear that the grandparent is not coming back. It is difficult for children to keep looking for the return of a grandparent when they have been told that they have just gone away. Sometimes they even imagine that they have made the grandparent angry and made them go away.

2. *Help them remember.* Often children have short memories and may become distressed when they cannot remember what their grandparent looked like. Giving them a photograph of their own can be helpful. They may want to write down a favorite memory of their grandparent or draw pictures of things they did together. A little scrapbook might be appropriate.

3. *Encourage them to talk about feelings.* Children have extraordinary imaginations and may have strange images about

what is happening to their grandparent or where their grandparent is. Children's tears affect adults, and when children cry adults often cry, too. They need to feel sad and be able to cry without worrying that their tears make other people sad. If the grandparent has been active right up until the time of death, or if the death was sudden, children may think that they or someone else caused it. If children hear adults in the guilt cycle talking about the death and wondering if they should have done something, the children may become angry at the adults for letting their grandparent die. Let them know that death happens to all people and no one causes it. Also reassure them that most people die when they are old so the children do not begin to fear their own death.

WHEN TO WORRY

The cycles of grief can be hard, and at times adult children may feel their surviving parent is stuck in one part of the cycle. Because the cycle repeats itself in various intensities, the primary symptom of an abnormal grief process is that the cycle is not moving. The older parent is exhibiting the same emotions and behaviors over an extended period of time, such as a several-week span of intense sadness. Grief is expressed in a variety of emotions—grateful remembering one day, anger the next, sadness the next. One counselor, Dan Blazer, has listed several abnormal grief reactions (Blazer 1990, 208-10).

Prolonged or unresolved grief. A number of symptoms might be associated with prolonged grief, such as guilt regarding the circumstances surrounding the loss and anger at the people, like health-care professionals, associated with the death. While both guilt and anger are emotions connected with grief, either one without the other might be a danger sign. If the cycle of grieving does not move along, depression often results. In some cases the health and longevity of the surviving parent is at stake.

Increased activity without sense of loss. The bereaved surviving parent exhibits a zeal for activities and begins making rash decisions or becomes unusually adventuresome. This constant activity helps keep the surviving parent from thinking about his or her loss. The parent cannot sit and cry for the deceased because there is never time to slow down long enough to sit.

Taking on the symptoms of the deceased spouse. The desire to identify with the lost spouse, and perhaps follow him or her in death, can be expressed in persistent complaints of the symptoms of the lost person. Doctors should be made aware of the cause of death of the deceased spouse, but they must also be sure to not dismiss the symptoms out of hand. Every appropriate medical intervention should be made.

Social isolation. In this reaction, the bereaved older parent has difficulty initiating any social activity and shows little response to the efforts of others to involve him or her. A cycle develops when the surviving parent has rebuffed family and friends so often that they stop making contact and the surviving parent becomes even more isolated.

POSSIBILITIES AND LOVE

Wherever the surviving parent is in the grief cycle and whether the grief is normal or abnormal, the important gifts adult children can give him or her are possibilities and love. The assurance that the future will be less painful and that there is always a new day coming can break through the guilt, anger, and sadness. The assurance of love is also important. The surviving parent has lost the physical presence of someone who loved him or her dearly, above all others. Adult children cannot and should not try to replace that love, but the assurance of a child's continued love comforts the loss of a spouse's love.

REACTING TO THE GRIEVING PARENT

The presence of loved ones helps to comfort the loss of a spouse. The first part of helping a grieving parent is being available.

1. *Be available.* This may not mean being there all the time. Time to cry in private, to remember and grieve alone, is essential. When being alone begins to crowd in on the grieving parent, knowing how to find company is essential to his or her well-being. A regularly scheduled phone call is helpful. Older parents look forward to the phone call and know it is coming. They enjoy not only the call but the anticipation. The same is true of visits. The pleasure of looking forward to the visit is almost as satisfying as the visit itself.

2. *Don't stop a grieving parent from crying.* When surviving parents cry, their children often try to comfort them and tell them not to cry. There are different kinds of tears. Some crying relieves the tension of grief by expressing sadness and loss. At other times the tears contribute to the anxiety by making the crying person feel guilty or self-conscious. It is important to let grieving persons decide what is good for them. Maybe crying is what they need most; maybe not. Letting their comfort level be the guide, instead of one's own comfort level, is difficult. It is also important for surviving parents to see their adult children cry. It confirms they are not alone in their grief and that the spouse they loved was loved by others.

3. *Help the grieving parent to remember.* While the sharp pain of loss makes remembering difficult, it is usually helpful in the long term. Often wakes and other funeral-related gatherings turn into sessions of remembering. When sadness is overwhelming, remembering specific sayings or familiar actions of the lost parent sometimes helps to alleviate the sadness. One woman sends a card to her widowed mother on every holiday with a story she remembers about something her father did or said. Her mother looks forward to these cards.

4. *Let your parent see your grief when appropriate.* The old saying that misery loves company is true for grief. Grief shared does seem easier. Often surviving parents will want to comfort their grieving children and in that comforting receive care for themselves. Parents never stop being parents.

When the first parent dies, the surviving parent becomes even more important to the adult children. They may want to become more involved in the parent's life and to be sure that the memories and experiences of their parents' generation are not lost. The next chapter discusses saying a final goodbye, terminal illness, and claiming the family heritage.

A Word for the Faithful. The sharp pain of grief is a reflection of the depth of love. The best gift that a surviving parent or adult child can receive is shared grief and shared memories. Remember that faith does not erase grief but transforms it into love, longing, and hope.

A Prayer for Older Parents. Dear God, help me to know that as I experience loss and loneliness, you bring me comfort and hope. Give me grace and faith to face the difficult times and surround me with people who love me. Amen.

A Prayer for Adult Children of Older Parents. Dear God, remind me every day of your love and comfort and show me ways that I can pass your love and comfort on to my parents. Help me to be patient with their greater need for company and to share my own grief with them. Amen.

CHAPTER 8

QUALITY GOODBYES

Last night my mother came to my room from heaven. I know it was probably a dream, but she was so real. It might have been an angel. She said that it was good where I was going and that my father, my brother, and the little daughter who died so many years ago were waiting. Everyone talks of seeing a tunnel. I saw a bridge. The water beneath was clear blue and the sky was brilliant with light. I was just going to walk over and then she would hug me and I could hold my little daughter. Yes, death is going to be all right. An adventure, a journey, a joining. I am going to another home.

—William, 78, retired contractor dying of throat cancer

William is close to death. Like many persons at this stage he has come to believe that his death will be a positive experience, although he is sad to leave his wife and children. If he could live without his disease, he would be glad to go on indefinitely. William is wise enough and has seen enough death and disease to know that he would rather die than remain in pain and discomfort, unable to live the kind of life he wants.

His wife, who has witnessed his decline and pain, is torn between knowing it is time to say goodbye and not wanting to let go. His children have a variety of feelings. One of his sons is still waiting for the miracle cure, not able to admit to himself that his father is dying. Two other sons are shutting off their sadness and trying to concentrate on their mother's needs. His daughter is hoping to give him the support that will allow him to let go and die. She shares his understanding of his impending death and cannot bear to see him suffer longer.

I'm not sure what my life will be like without him. I depend on him still to give me good advice and help me decide what to do in the world. But I would die myself if I could save him the painful death that seems to be ahead of him. He is afraid of the pain. I know that. Mom and I are going to talk again to the doctors about his pain relief. We feel like we are his fighters now. We have to be on the line for him.

—Barbara, 45, daughter of William

Many adult children become more active in their older parents' care as death approaches, especially if one parent is already deceased. When the last parent dies, a generation in the family also passes. Often dying parents want to know that life as they knew it and the contributions they made to their family will not be forgotten.

KNOWING DEATH IS COMING

As older parents enter the last stages of life, they face many assaults to their self-esteem through physical and mental changes. In spite of these adjustments, older adults usually retain whatever levels of self-worth they have developed in the course of their lives. If they are able to look upon their lives with a reasonable amount of satisfaction, they face death as the final stage of a good life. Their children can also help them view their lives from the perspective of the generation that is to carry on for them.

I have had such a great life. I started out plowing with a mule when I was eighteen. I survived World War II and married the most beautiful woman in the country. My children are all good people. They work hard, love one another, and have given me the most perfect grandchildren in the world. I am willing to die now before I lose my ability to see all this goodness in my life. I do not want to become a cranky, bitter old man. I don't want my children to see me as weak. I don't want to reach a place in life where I don't know who I am. It would be so unfair because I have had such happiness.

—Paul, 81, retired auto mechanic

Paul speaks for many older adults. He has a level of satisfaction with his life that is more important than an extra month or year of living without this satisfaction. He also knows that his final illness presents new needs for his spouse that may make them dependent on others for the first time since they were children. The American Health Care Association has published the pamphlet *Here's Help! Death and Dying* (undated), which identifies four categories of needs: physical, social, emotional, and religious or spiritual.

Physical. The dying need food, water, shelter, and comfort just as all people do. They probably have special needs related to their illness, such as relief from pain, help in moving around, or help in eating. They may need attention to adjust the room temperature or for other physical needs. Often the most critical need is to have an advocate in the medical system, as William's wife and daughter have become to him. They use their energy, persistence, and ability to understand the medical system to be sure that William receives the care he needs.

Social. Many dying patients fear abandonment, especially if their illness requires hospitalization that separates them from their usual support networks. It is imperative that adult children help their dying parents to maintain social contacts. Some friends and family find being with terminally ill persons very difficult, but their discomfort must be weighed against the need of the terminally ill person. Even contact by telephone or letter can be important.

The content of the contacts is also important. Terminally ill persons need a mixture of normal activities, such as playing cards or telling jokes, and activities that help them prepare for death, which might include talking about the past, making contact with people from their past with whom there is unfinished business, or talking about how they feel.

Emotional. Emotional needs can be complex. Terminally ill persons need to express appreciation, regret, and last goodbyes. They may also feel out of control of their lives and as if they have no choices left. These feelings can produce fear and the need for reassurance. They will grieve, feeling sadness, loss, anger, and guilt because they are leaving the ones they love.

Adult children will have some of the same emotional needs in connection with their dying parent. Tension can arise when the parent is feeling anger and the adult child is feeling a need for affection. The reverse is also true. There can be moments when the dying parent and adult child feel so connected that the moment is almost holy.

Religious or spiritual. These needs are quite personal and varied, but moments of feeling union with one's family, the universe, and God are a common desire. All people need to feel this spiritual unity, and many have religious beliefs in prayer that help them feel it.

I prayed with Daddy today. It was the first time we had prayed together, and me a grown man. It'll be our last, too. He's soon going to die. I wonder why I waited so long. We both needed it. It bound us together with God.

—Al, 62, son of William

There are many other kinds of religious and spiritual needs. Some faiths have certain prayers for the sick and dying; others have customs of sitting together with the dying. Adult children and their parents may disagree about religious matters. Even though children may find themselves torn at times between their faith and the desires of their parents, neither the adult children nor the parents should compromise their values and faith but rather work toward a middle ground.

I don't hold much to the faith any longer. My wife and children go to temple, and I guess I still believe. Dad, he wanted the prayers. I called the rabbi and made the arrangements, but I couldn't participate. It wouldn't have been right since I no longer pray myself. I waited outside. Dad was in tears when I came back into the room. I'm glad I called the rabbi. It was the right thing to do for him. I told my wife, though, that when I die she's just to hold my hand and let me go. Dad wouldn't have understood at all, so I didn't tell him.

—Herman, 56, son of Jacob, 87

STAGES OF ACCEPTANCE OF TERMINAL ILLNESS

Elisabeth Kübler-Ross, in *On Death and Dying*, explores stages of the dying process. Her belief is that most people facing death go through the stages in some form and that the families participate with them in this process.

Denial and isolation. When first confronted with the news that one has a terminal illness, denial protects the individual from the full impact of the news. Denial is often followed by loneliness and a sense of isolation. Adult children may experience denial and isolation as well when they learn of a parent's terminal illness. Denial is self-protecting. Either the terminally ill parent or the adult child may try to break the denial of the other prematurely, but it is best if the parent determines the timing for discussing the illness and events to come. One approach is for the child to say, "I know you are going to die from this illness, and I want to talk about it when you're ready."

Letting a patient work through the denial of terminal illness is different from not telling the patient that he or she is terminally ill. The stage of denial presumes that there has been open communication between medical staff, the dying parent, and the family. Secrets about the illness are not helpful. Most terminally ill persons are instinctively aware of the seriousness of their illness without being told. Open communication that tells the truth can be a relief.

Once the patient knows the truth, he or she backs away until ready to deal with it. It is this backing away from the truth that is called denial. Availability and patience are the gifts an adult child gives the parent at this stage.

Anger. The second stage is anger. This stage may be the most difficult for family and medical staff because the anger is directed not only at the disease but at everyone around the person who is ill. The younger the patient the more radical this stage may be. Older parents may find their anger is not so much at the eventual end of their disease, death, but at the kind of disease that is claiming their life.

I have always been afraid of cancer. I have watched family members die of cancer. I don't want to waste away and be in pain. I don't want to throw up all the time and lose my hair to chemotherapy. I don't want this disease. But it is going to kill me, and everything I have hoped to avoid I will face. So that's it. I said I wanted to drop dead of a heart attack, and instead God sends cancer. Thanks a lot.
—Grace, 78, retired teacher and colon cancer patient

Grace has hit on most of the points of anger. Anger at the kind of disease and the way she will die. Anger at God, whether or not she really believes God gave her colon cancer. Grace might also be angry at the doctors for not finding a way to cure her. She might be angry that it's a family-linked disease. She might blame herself for her illness and for not taking better care of herself. She may even be angry at her children because they will go on living after she is dead and she will not be with them.

In dealing with misplaced anger, adult children have only

two choices: take the anger and hang in with the parent, or walk away and try to reestablish contact after their parent is through this stage. Most choose to take the anger as best as they can, sometimes silently and sometimes responding from their own hurt and anger. Forgiveness and understanding are the gifts adult children can give their dying parents during this stage.

Bargaining. In this stage the patient attempts to postpone death by making bargains with the medical staff, with the family, with oneself, and with God. Kübler-Ross tells of one woman who begged the staff to keep her alive until her son was married. After her son married she returned to the hospital and immediately reminded the staff she had another son (Kübler-Ross 1993, 72-73). The bargaining can go on and on, but the reality of the disease eventually ends this stage. There is no real bargain that can keep death away.

Adult children are not immune to bargaining. They may promise God never to do that one horrible thing for which they think God may be punishing them. The reality is that all the bargaining in the world will not change the disease. The gift adult children give their parents in this stage is listening. As the reality breaks through the bargaining, both the dying parent and the adult children have the same next stage, depression. When the bargaining ends the crying begins.

Depression. This depression is sometimes a preparation for the grief of the separation that death will bring. The intensity and duration vary, but the substance is the same. It is sad to leave loved ones behind.

I cry all the time these days. I see a child and I cry because I have a great-grandchild I am leaving. I cry when I see the sunshine because I remember how my son and I played in the sunshine. I cry when I hear lots of songs because they all have memories. I even cry at television commercials. I was worried about how much I was crying, but my son said, "Mom, you can't cry forever." He meant I had to stop sometime and when I did he would still be beside me.

—Grace

The depth of these feelings are sometimes surprising for both dying parents and their adult children. The depth of the sadness is in proportion to the depth of the love. The gift adult children can give their parents in this stage is to see the depression and the tears for what they are, expressions of love.

Grief and love are two sides of the same coin. Only people who love deeply grieve deeply, and grief is a small price to pay for love.

—Grace

Acceptance. Acceptance is not necessarily a happy stage but rather a peaceful one that is more void of feelings, a resting stage. Often it is accompanied by more sleep, by quieter conversations, and less battling against the disease, one's family, and medical personnel. It is not an abandonment of hope. Most terminally ill persons hold out hope to continue living, a miracle from somewhere, until days or hours before their death.

Hope is a necessity of living. Hope pushes toward the future, a new day. For people who believe in some kind of life after death, hope even lasts beyond death. For others it lives in the memories, values, and personality that the dying parent has left behind. The gifts that adult children give their dying parents in this stage are assurance that who they are and the things they valued will not be forgotten and encouragement for the parent to take care of last things.

HEALING OLD WOUNDS

For many dying parents and their adult children, the knowledge of terminal illness provides a push toward reconciliation of past hurts and misunderstandings.

Misunderstandings. Sometimes seemingly little things keep bothering family members long after they have happened. When older parents know they are dying, it is important that they leave with these misunderstandings straightened out.

My father missed lots of events in my life because he was working, and I used to think it was because I was less important than his work. Yesterday, as I sat by his hospital bed, he suddenly said to me, "I only worked so much because I loved you so much. I wish you would understand. I was trying so hard to take care of my family." My father hadn't told me he loved me in years. I started to cry, and he thought I was mad at him. We talked and talked and worked it out. Now that he's dying we're finally talking. It's not fair.

—Sarah, 56, daughter of Jacob

Sarah is right that it is not fair. Adult children whose parents are both alive might consider letting the lesson Sarah is learning affect their relationship with the parent that is not ill. Perhaps Sarah can talk to her mother about the misunderstandings and small hurts that have never been settled before her mother is critically ill. Sarah's father may be, in his way, asking for forgiveness for the hurts he believes he has caused. This is also an opportunity for adult children to absolve their parents of real or imagined hurts and give their parents a gift of peace.

Outstanding questions. Adult children may have outstanding questions about their lives, and the dying parent is the best person to answer such questions. Perhaps there is information about grandparents and great-grandparents that the newer generations would like to have. Maybe it is as simple as learning about a parent's childhood or as complex as why the parent holds the religious beliefs that have been part of the family life.

Adult children have this last chance to get answers, and often the questions give parents a chance to relive their past, share their values, and pass on their wisdom. The respect this shows is a lasting gift.

Laughter. Most people love to laugh, and one is never too sick or too old to live without humor.

My mom was always laughing and causing us to laugh. She loved a funny story, even about herself, and she loved to play little practical jokes on us. So I decided this death business was getting far too serious. While she was in radiology having yet another test of some kind, I put a rubber frog on her pillow. The nurse that brought her back jumped a foot. My mother laughed for ten minutes. I hadn't heard her laugh for so long. The frog sits in one of the plants now to remind us to laugh. She said all the plants and flowers look more like a funeral, but the frog reminds us both that for now, for this moment on this day, Mom is very much alive.

—Deborah, 42, daughter of Marion, 67, dying of cancer

Rubber frogs may not be appropriate for everyone, but laughter can help more than most people realize. Perhaps an old friend can be brought to see the terminally ill patient, someone who can make the patient laugh. Sometimes the antics of a grandchild or great-grandchild can cheer an older parent. If hospital officials realize that a patient is dying, they can find ways to be lenient on visitation rules. Adult children can ask specifically for such help.

Saying "I love you." As strange at it seems, those whom people love the most hear them say it the least. People who live together day to day might forget the importance of saying "I love you" out loud. There might be an unspoken family rule that Mom and Dad do not usually say "I love you," so no one says it to them.

I am forty-nine years old, and today for a moment I was so jealous of my six-year-old granddaughter that I was ashamed. She crawled right up in my father's lap and said, "I love you, Papaw." He said, "I love you, too." I wanted to cry. I have wanted for years to hear my dad say he loved me. He was always too

tough, too reserved. But that little girl didn't know the rule, and so she broke it. I took a deep breath and said, "I love you, too, Daddy." He just nodded. Then his eyes filled with tears and he said, "I love you." My heart nearly broke. Why do we obey all these unwritten rules? Maybe I could have heard it years ago if I had only been brave enough to say it first.
    —Jenny, 49, daughter of Melvin, 78, dying of lung cancer

Talking to a dying parent sometimes requires an incredible amount of courage. Jenny had to risk that her father would not respond, and the absence of the words would have been even more painful and powerful than before. Most persons who know they are dying want to be sure their love is understood, though some are never able to say all they need or want to say. The risk adult children take to be sure their parents have the chance to say "I love you" is a gift to both parent and child.

RISK TAKING AND BELIEVING IN GOD

A challenge to Christians as death approaches is whether or not to communicate things that have never been said. Some things may be better left unsaid—grievances that should have been forgiven long ago are better turned over to God. It can be self-serving to pour out lists of past hurts on someone who needs forgiveness and reconciliation. It may also be absolutely necessary to talk about the injuries of the past. Courage is required to ask God, "Why am I feeling the need to talk about this? Is it something I should forgive and let go? Is it something that must be spoken?"

When there are difficult things to be said, there is a risk. Some people facing death change longstanding patterns of dealing with conflict and want to resolve differences. Others remain true to their personalities and to their interpretation of relationships to the end. Christians may find the risk of being hurt by a rebuff or further conflict worth taking when forgiveness and grace may be the outcome instead.

I remember the first time my father said he loved me. I was forty-two years old. He was facing serious cancer surgery and didn't think he would live. I still feel my heart breaking as he said the words. I longed for them for so long, but in the end they changed nothing because I had always known he loved me. The words were confirmation of something he had proven over and over. I will never know what they cost him to say, but he knew I wanted to hear them.

—Sarah

Sam did not die in surgery but several months later, and without repeating the words again. However, as he died he whispered to his wife, "Tell the kids I love them." They were always on his mind. Christians need to say the "I love you" that they haven't said. The "I forgive you" and the "We will be together again" also need to be expressed.

Paul told the Romans in his letter that nothing could separate them from the love of God. This is the promise that Christians claim when approaching the tumultuous time of grief. The risk taking of talking through unfinished business is to be seen in light of this promise—God's love is supreme and above all.

> No, in all these things we are more than conquerors through him who loved us. For I am convinced that neither death, nor life, nor angels, nor rulers, nor things present, nor things to come, nor powers, nor height, nor depth, nor anything else in all creation, will be able to separate us from the love of God in Christ Jesus our Lord. (Romans 8:37-39)

NEED TO TALK

Although some terminally ill persons become withdrawn and do not want to talk as they draw nearer to death, most feel a strong need to talk. This need to talk can be expressed in several ways. One revolves around sharing current experiences.

Sharing current experiences. Because most older parents are moderately healthy until their last illness, the day-to-day assaults of disease on their bodies can be hard to cope with emotionally and spiritually as well as physically. Talking to someone about the latest round of tests or the frustration with a new disability associated with the illness can be important. It also helps adult children understand exactly what their parents are going through and perhaps enables them to let go of their parents when death comes. If some older children in a family live far from the parents and see them on an infrequent basis, some arrangement for them to talk to the dying parent is important. Not only does it bring the family closer together, it gives the absent adult children a glimpse of the reality of their parent's illness.

Advocacy with the medical system often grows out of these discussions of the current situation. Parents who share their continual upset at the indignities and discomfort that often accompany medical care can encourage their children to intervene for them when possible.

As soon as I saw my mother I knew she was unhappy and in pain. I asked her to tell me about the last few days when I had not been with her. It seems the nurse who had been so good about caring for her was on vacation and somehow she didn't feel she was getting the same care from the staff. I witnessed it firsthand when they left her on the bedpan for about thirty minutes. I wanted to help her myself, but she didn't want me to. It would have embarrassed her. She also didn't get prescribed pain medication on time. I realize they were shorthanded and didn't blame them, but I just couldn't handle this. I talked to the shift supervisor and she was helpful. Things got better. Then I talked to the doctor and he increased her pain medication. It is a trade-off. She sleeps more but is more comfortable. Trade-offs are what life is all about now. She traded the misery of chemotherapy for a few more months of

*life. She trades her sharp mind to have both it and the pain
dulled. I want to be sure the trade-offs are the best we can get.*
—Ellie, 45, daughter of Elsa, 76, dying of a brain tumor

The stories are not always easy to hear, and adult children
may need to find someone to talk to also. The sharing of the
story not only makes it more real, breaking through denial, but
makes it more bearable by allowing the expression of sadness
and grief.

Long lost stories. Some of the need to talk is about the past.
The dying parent may repeat several times important stories of
their childhood, stories the adult children have heard many
times before. The content of these stories give important messages about what the dying parent values. To listen to values
and desires hidden in the content and affirm those is a gift to
the dying parent.

Some stories may not be familiar. Approaching death, in
most mentally alert parents, brings a review of their life. They
go over the details of their life and share these details with their
children. They tell their adult children what they want them to
remember.

Family secrets. In a minority of instances there is an overwhelming family secret that must come out in order for the parent to die peacefully. Some of these secrets can catch adult
children off guard because they contain negative information.
Some adult children have discovered they were adopted or that
their mother was really a stepmother or their father a stepfather.

Telling the truth, even though it is painful, may be the best
step the dying parent can take in bringing about reconciliation
with his or her family. A secret has been kept because of the
expectation of a negative reaction, and the adult children may
react with anger, shock, frustration, or all of these emotions.
Telling the truth about their feelings is as important to the
process of reconciliation as telling the secret. Sometimes
healthy family members make the mistake of thinking they

must always be cheerful, positive, and long-suffering, but this is not true. They must be honest, understanding, and willing to listen in as much as they are able.

I had no idea that my grandfather had deserted my grandmother or that the man I knew as a grandfather was really my grandfather's brother who had married grandmother after the desertion. I wonder what else is secret. I wonder why it is important that I know this now, that my grandfather was not my grandfather. He is dead and grandmother is dying. I told her I was angry she hadn't told me and she hadn't been fair to lie to me. I really yelled at her, and the nurse told me to leave. The next day Grandmother seemed better than before. The yelling hadn't hurt her nearly as much as the telling had helped her. I'm still mad.

—Carolyn, 22, granddaughter of Cora, 78,
dying of congestive heart failure

There are some illnesses, such as some heart conditions, that make it advisable for patients to have as little upset as possible. However, if dying parents or grandparents choose to be upset in the service of telling the stories they need to tell, then that is their choice. They may not be as concerned about hastening death by a week or so as they are about dying with a secret untold. The gifts of listening, trying to understand, and assuring of love are important to both dying parents and their children.

Planning the farewell. Some people have planned their funeral down to the last detail, knowing clearly what they want and do not want. However, adult children may need to ask their dying parents what they want. Should the service be religious? Are there specific readings or songs to be included? Do they want a special service, such as cremation?

Farewells are for the living to begin to let go and separate from the physical presence of their loved ones. Honoring the loved one's wishes is usually a final gift that adult children can give their parents. Often people are reluctant to talk about the final farewell because it seems morbid or makes the certainty of death even more real. Dying patients, especially those who have reached the stage of acceptance, are often relieved to talk about their final farewell. Most have definite ideas and desires.

I want all my family and friends to gather and laugh and eat and celebrate my life. The more people wearing red the better. I like red. It's a passionate color. I want them to tell stories about me and have wonderful memories of our times together. Then a prayer and a tear as they lower me into the ground. No dirges, no wailing, please! I have nothing to regret except that I can't live forever.

—Amanda, 84, homemaker

If all the last wishes are impossible to honor, talking about them will help get through the painful last goodbye. Amanda's children might choose to wear red, to have only a graveside service, and even to throw a great feast for all her friends and family, but they could hardly promise not to weep.

PLANNING TO REMEMBER

Dying patients want to be remembered. One way that adult children help their parents to say goodbye to this life is to assure them that they will be remembered.

Reminiscing groups. "Reminiscing groups" were formed by some therapists (Brody and Semel 1993, 14-19) as a way to help residents in nursing facilities remember their lives. The same idea might be applied to family groups. Perhaps a dying parent has brothers and sisters still alive. An adult child might plan to reunite the family for the purpose of talking about their lives as children in a family.

Another group could be made up of the children of a dying parent to remind the parent of their lives as children. These planned groups of "remembering" might help terminally ill parents who are finding talking difficult begin to open up. If parents are unable to talk, it gives them a group to talk for them.

Life review. The old television show *This Is Your Life* was popular because it gave viewers a glimpse into the nonfamous portions of a famous person's life. A life review with the dying parent can be helpful in facilitating talking and also in assuring the parent that he or she will be remembered. The parent may have details of his or her early life that the adult children have never heard.

Photographs and tapes. Walking through antique stores one often sees old family photos, unlabeled and unclaimed. While it may be true that all the family is dead, it is more likely that no one knows who the family members are. Adult children may want to make an effort to take out the boxes of photos and put names and dates on as many as possible while their parents can tell them who is who. The photographs will undoubtedly bring out stories and family history.

Some adult children choose to visit older relatives as well as their own parents with a tape recorder to tape family histories.

The generation that is the older adult population has seen the most remarkable changes in history. These adults have witnessed the coming of the modern era. They have gone from plowing with a mule to seeing a man walk on the moon. To lose their thoughts, feelings, and observations would mean to lose the wisdom of a special generation.

To acknowledge that their older parents' thoughts, feelings, and knowledge are important as they say goodbye to their world, their family, and friends may be the most important gift that adult children can give.

A Word for the Faithful. All things pass and new things come to be. Whenever a new stage or phase of life is entered, it is an adjustment. For adult children whose parents have died, the new phase is one of being the seniors in their families, and whatever qualities and values they showed with their parents will probably be the ones shown to them. The great commandment to love others as self comes full circle.

A Prayer for Adult Children of Older Parents. Dear God, as I become the oldest generation in my family, help me to accept the changes in my life and the caring and compassion of my children with grace and dignity. Give me hope and faith. Amen.

CONCLUSION

I remember visiting my father in the hospital during one of my annual trips home. I saw him sitting on the bed, almost a stranger because he had lost so much weight and the deep tan in his farmer face was gone. I realized he was embarrassed by his illness. I was also filled with the certainty that in looking at him sitting on the edge of that hospital bed I was also looking at my future. I would someday be frail, pale, and embarrassed at my loss of independence.

Perhaps at the heart of the discomfort and frustration we adult children feel when faced with our aging parents is the certainty that we too will age. Maybe we feel too keenly our own limitations and have begun to recognize the beginning arthritis in the knee we injured so long ago.

All of the promises God makes to us are just as real at twenty, at forty, and at eighty. Nothing can separate us from the love of God in Jesus Christ—not age, not responsibilities, not disappointments, not changes, not grief. If we, adult children and our older parents, can learn to depend upon the love of God, we will have that certainty when everything else becomes uncertain.

REFERENCES

American Association of Retired Persons. 1991. *A Profile of Older Americans: 1991*. Washington, D.C.: Administration on Aging. U.S. Department of Health and Human Services

American Health Care Association. Undated. *Here's Help! Death and Dying*. Washington, D.C.

Blazer, D. 1990. *Emotional Problems in Later Life*. New York: Springer Publishing Company.

Brody, C. M., and V. G. Semel. 1993. *Strategies for Therapy with the Elderly*. New York: Springer Publishing Company.

Grambs, J. D. 1989. *Women Over Fifty*. New York: Springer Publishing Company.

Himmelfarb, S., and S. A. Murrell. 1984. "The Prevalence and Correlation of Anxiety Symptoms in Older Adults." *The Journal of Psychology*, 116:159-67.

Kahana, R. J., and G. L. Bibring. 1964. "Personality Types in Medical Management" in E. N. Zinber, ed., *Psychiatry and Medical Practice in a General Hospital*. New York: International University Press.

Kübler-Ross, E. 1993. *On Death and Dying*. New York: Macmillan Publishing Company.

MacDonald, C. B. 1993. "Loss and Bereavement" in R. J. Wicks, et.al., eds., *Clinical Handbook of Pastoral Counseling*, Volume 1. New York: Integration Books, Paulist Press.

Muslin, H. L. 1992. *The Psychotherapy of the Elderly Self.* New York: Brunner Mozel.

Rosenberg, M. 1979. *Concerning the Self.* New York: Basic Books.

Select Committee on Aging, U.S. House of Representatives. 1987. Washington, D.C.: U.S. Government Printing Office, Committee Publication No. 100–631.

Waters, E., and J. Goodman. 1990. *Empowering Older Adults.* San Francisco: Jossey-Bass Publishers.